R I TRICKER

EFFECTIVE INFORMATION MANAGEMENT

Developing
Information Systems
Strategies

VNR VAN NOSTRAND REINHOLD COMPANY

Copyright © 1982 by R.I. Tricker

Library of Congress Catalog Card Number: 84–3596
ISBN: 0–442–28307–5

Manufactured in the United States of America

Published by Van Nostrand Reinhold Company Inc.
135 West 50th Street
New York, New York 10020

Van Nostrand Reinhold Company Limited
Molly Millars Lane
Wokingham, Berkshire RG11 2PY, England

Van Nostrand Reinhold
480 Latrobe Street
Melbourne, Victoria 3000, Australia

Macmillan of Canada
Division of Gage Publishing Limited
164 Commander Boulevard
Agincourt, Ontario MIS 3C7, Canada

15 14 13 12 11 10 9 8 7 6 5 4 3 2 1

Library of Congress Cataloging in Publication Data

Tricker, R. Ian (Robert Ian)
  Effective information management.

  Includes indes.
  1. Management information systems. I. Title.
T58.6.T68   1984   658.4'038   84–3596
ISBN 0–442–28307–5

Contents

Introduction

The need for information in the modern organisation has never been greater. The provision of data has never been wider. But whilst decision makers face a surfeit of data; there is a paucity of information.

Providing more data, more accurately, more quickly and making it more readily accessible does not, of itself, provide more information; even less does it produce better informed executives.

For some, telecommunications and computers offer a solution to the information problem. But those organisations that are well advanced in this area find that the technical and operational answer can have dramatic strategic consequences. Technology has run ahead of management's ability to use it. Opportunities in new organisation structures and management styles, facilitated by modern information systems, have outstripped managers' ability to imagine the alternatives.

The time has come for managers to reassert control over their information and their organisation.

Around the world decision-makers face growing complexity: there are more factors to be taken into account. The interests of more people have to be recognised: there are wider demands for access to information, accountability and involvement. Increasing scale and concentration, interdependence and internationalisation, add new dimensions to the problems of management co-ordination and control. Yet, in the midst of this, the executive has to act.

Management, which used to involve responses to the pressures of change, has become the process of causing change. No longer able to see the future as an outgrowth of the past, information has become crucial. It is the link in organisational relationships, the basis of managerial control and the stimulus for imaginative strategy.

Content: For nearly twenty years MIS (management information systems) has been thought about as the application of computers to business and administrative processes. In business schools MIS courses have been taught on the basis of computer-assisted applications.

This book provides a completely new orientation. Information system developments are shown to be organisational developments. Senior managers are not passive patrons of system developments; they must recognise strategic implications and determine strategic directions.

This is not a book about computers. A manager does not have to be an electronics engineer to use the telephone. He does, however, have to appreciate the available services and know what is required of him. The book does emphasise management's responsibility for organisation structure, management planning, co-ordination and control, and the formulation of strategy in the light of the technological potential for handling information. It will indicate many of the key questions that senior executives should be discussing and the knowledge that managers should have on the subject.

Technological opportunities abound—stand-alone minis and micros, intelligent terminals front-ending other systems, teleprocessing, personal computers, distributed intelligence, external data-banks, accessing new sources of knowledge, the electronic office . . . no longer are the issues technical. We now face questions about the real managerial and organisational needs of the enterprise. Such matters go far beyond a pre-occupation with cost-effective computing.

What are the implications for organisation structure and management style? If we tend to centralise the information systems, shall we tend to centralise the organisation structure and management controls? If we give operational units more autonomy, must we decentralise the records leading to wide-spread data-processing?

Where should decisions about information systems be taken? At Head Office—to ensure compatibility, scale economies and sensible co-operation; or at the organisation's periphery where involvement and motivation might be encouraged? How much autonomy do we want to give the departments, divisions and subsidiaries around the world?

Where should files be located? Who should have access? Will other parties, trade unions or consumer groups, for example, acquire rights of access to such files? Are changes taking place in the organisation's environment that may make new demands for information?

Issues such as these are facing senior executives throughout the advanced world. There are no panaceas for organisational design, no simple techniques waiting to be applied. Much more is at stake. We are concerned with the very strategy, structure and style of the enterprise.

The issues apply to all significant organisations today—business and building society, union and university, hospital and hat shop—all need their information systems strategy.

Purpose: The book has been written for the business executive and the public sector administrator who want to understand the managerial implications of new information technologies. It will enable them to appreciate the issues, the opportunities and the risks. It could lead to new organisational initiatives and better informed, more intelligent, organisations in practice.

It will also be useful in post-experience management courses and MBA programmes; and be of interest to all thinking people who want to know something of the potential for new information and organisational strategies.

Origins: For some years I have been leading executive seminars around the world—the United States and Canada, the United Kingdom and Europe, South Africa, Australia and New Zealand. These discussions of key issues and opportunities, challenges and constraints, have provided valuable background material. Then, for over ten years, I have been working, at board level, in business and public sector organisations, with small groups working on the improvement of their organisational and information strategies. Thus the thinking in the book is rooted in practical case experience.

The genesis of the work, and the conceptual, theoretical underpinnings go back further, to the time when I was Professor of Information Systems at the University of Warwick.

The opportunity to undertake the study underlying this book has been provided by three organisations—

Nuffield College, Oxford, where I hold a Research Fellowship, and which provided a location for the work,

The Oxford Centre for Management Studies, where I hold a Professorial Fellowship, which thus provided financial support for me during the period of study, and

The Corporate Policy Group, Oxford, which I direct, and which provided the research support.

I acknowledge, with many thanks, my gratitude to the Warden and Fellows, Director and Council, and Trustees concerned.

Acknowledgements: Over the years I have developed a network of scholars, consultants and practitioners in the field whose friendly advice and comment has extended my thinking and widened my knowledge. To them all I am most grateful.

But, inevitably, the responsibility for the conclusions drawn here rest with the author—and for their implementation and effect with the reader.

R. I. Tricker
Oxford 1982

1
The Strategic Significance of Information Systems
•why all organisations should have an information systems strategy

'Top management in this company has always been involved in the development of our computer systems. What I now realise is that patronage is not enough. The top executives have to be committed to systems planning: the effects are now at our level.'
Chief Executive Officer of a major multinational corporation

'We're spending millions; how do I know whether we're taking the right decisions and using our computers and telecommunications properly. Yet we are totally dependent on them now.'
Managing Director of a large private company

'I sometimes wish we could get back to pencil and paper—at least things would slow up.'
Administrator in a hospital group

Three Decades of Computing
The first decade of computing, in business and public administration, was focused primarily on existing operations in the enterprise. The emphasis was on supporting the on-going activities.

In the '60s the manager responsible for developing and running computer systems spent his time on technical and operational problems, of which there were plenty. His system would be based around a central processing unit and the applications would involve the processing of batches of transactions—for example, in payroll, invoicing, inventory records, maintenance scheduling and so on.

5

In managerial terms the investment, in cash and many man-years of effort, was justified if it reduced costs and contributed to the effectiveness of the organisation as a whole. Most computer systems in these days were approved on the basis of reduced staff, in the wages office for example; or improved cash management, by lowering inventories or faster billing for example. Top management commitment was necessary at the investment appraisal stage and to give the system-analyst function the authority to introduce the changes. Proper project management of the systems analysis, design and implementation was vital, as was efficient management of the day to day computer operations. But the real issues, the things that dominated his thinking and took his time were operational and technical. What he was doing had little strategic significance.

The decade of the '70s saw widespread developments in large tele-processing systems and remote terminals. The computer-assisted systems began to straddle the existing functional boundaries of organisation—and in some cases to change them. The systems executive found himself involved in questions of structure—where the organisational boundaries were to be redrawn, where the locus and responsibility for decisions should lie, where files should be held and who had the right to access or update them. The issue was often seen, in that glorious oversimplification that we shall return to in chapter 6, as a 'matter of centralisation or decentralisation'.

Asked, in the mid '70s to identify the issues most likely to affect information system development in the next ten years, a group of senior system executives identified three:

... internal organisational problems

... involvement in the organisation by third party interests

and ... the impact of factors external to the business.

Note the absence of any concern for the problems of technology or systems methodology which would have dominated such a peer-group discussion in the '60s. The executives felt that technology was ahead of management's ability to recognise the opportunities and appreciate the real issues.

Today we are into the third decade of computing. Now the technology permeates all corners of the enterprise. Indeed it is misleading to think just of computing, because related telecommunications and a whole range of electronic equipment, computer and micro-processor assisted, have to be considered. The technological potential, as we shall see in chapter 4, is enormous.

Increasingly now we find it is the users who are forcing the pace in system developments, and the data processing staff who counsel caution. Top executives, riding the learning curve with gusto, no longer show visitors the company computer in its glass enclosure. They expect cost-effective performance and significant contributions to the enterprise from telecommunications and computing.

Nevertheless, the majority of top executives in today's enterprises did have their formulative managerial experiences before computers were invented. Although increasingly those with computing experience are finding their way into the executive suite and the boardroom. But there is a danger. Computing can still be thought of as a contribution to the way the business is run—not as an alternative way of running the business.

Herein lie the dangers and the opportunities to be explored further. The key issues are operational no longer: they are strategic. To emphasise this point consider the strategic significance of information systems in a few case examples.

The Strategic Significance of Information Systems

The impact on marketing strategy

- The board of an Australian insurance company planned to introduce a new type of policy. To promote it they wanted to identify all of their existing policy-holders, between certain ages, who did not have the relevant cover. Although the data was available, it was on different files and the association of data proved difficult and expensive. A competitor launched a similar policy ahead of them and badly affected their market plan. 'Our system is just about set like concrete', commented the Managing Director afterwards.

There is a price to be paid for flexibility in access to data, but the cost needs to be set in the context of the corporate whole. If the information is vital to the achievement of a major marketing strategy, the value may far outweigh the cost on the data-processing budget.

Other companies are integrating their marketing strategies with their system plans in a more positive way.

- Another insurance company, this time in the United States, has linked each of their agents' small computers to their own system. Initially this was done to create an information network for the immediate calculation and presentation of guides for life assurance. Now they are considering whether to offer to undertake the agents' bookkeeping and maintain their files. It is a service far ahead of anything the competition can offer. They have succeeded in creating an on-line marketing network.

- The American Express Company are developing a US wide network to provide terminal access, in every branch office and agency, to all air-line reservation systems and the company's own travel and hotel services. Regular customers will have their travel requirements maintained on files in the system. Such a system will become a fundamental component of the way that company does business. American Express will not market its system to other travel companies, as the company believes it will give them a definite marketing advantage. Savings in agents' time of around 50% are expected, enabling them to concentrate on counselling and selling travel services.

- A leading car manufacturer in Europe has introduced a car inventory record system throughout its network of main dealers. Again the system is on-line and, through it, an agent can locate any car with the specifications and colour required by a customer. Inventories can be managed more efficiently and sales significantly increased.

The impact on production and technological strategies

In some mature, manufacturing companies business development and growth come less from product or marketing innovations than from technological change in the production processes. The massive reduction in unit cost to be achieved by automated production methods with high volume is well illustrated in the Japanese strategy to acquire a large share of Western markets in watches, calculators, TV and home electronic equipment, motor cycles, motor cars and, in the future, computers and office electronics.

Significantly the information system is frequently the driving component of such advanced production technology.

- In the Metro car production plant of British Leyland there is widespread use of automation and robotics. Sensors on the production equipment are linked, through micro-processors, to the central information system which monitors the logistics of the plant and controls the automated warehouses. There is no other way that the productivity level, necessary for the success of this operation, can be achieved.

The financial implications of system developments can go right to the heart of the cost structure of the business. Consider the New York Times:

- In the New York Times the paper's reporters now type their copy directly on to a terminal which enters it into the system where it is available for all subsequent editing. The paper is made up from the computer record and the type set by laser beam, operating at 1000 lines a minute, compared with three lines a minute on a conventional linotype machine. The copy can be transmitted by wire, radio and satellite to different locations. A breakdown or dispute in the Manhatten plant, and production can be run in New Jersey.

  Reported savings have been significant. The classified advertisements of a Sunday edition, which used to take three days to set, is now composed by the computer based system in less than 30 minutes. Staff in the linotype department have been halved. The system was accepted by the printers' union after a series of

confrontations. The impact on the financial strategy
of the paper may well be the difference between
success and failure in the longer term.

The impact on financial strategy

The proportion of the annual expenditure on communications in most organisations has increased significantly in recent
years and is still increasing. The entrepreneurial enterprise spends
a minimal amount. Increasing bureaucracy adds further expense.
Larger organisations multiply the need for expenditure to co-
ordinate and communicate internally. Annual budgets for telecommunication and computing now run into tens or hundreds
of millions in large companies. If the costs of executive time,
travel, meetings, mail and similar communication costs are added
the proportion of the revenue of the enterprise consumed may
approach 30% in a service industry and 10 or 15% in a manufacturing industry. Clearly costs of this order are a significant
component of any financial strategy. The benefits of such expenditure have to be shown.

- A major international company, in the chemical and
  pharmaceutical field, operated through subsidiary
  companies round the world. The management policy
  had always been that each subsidiary was responsible
  for generating profits against an annual plan and con-
  tributing an annual dividend in cash to corporate
  funds. Since the company introduced a global reporting system, cash and funds flow have increasingly been
  controlled from the Corporate Treasurer's office. As
  the Company President says:

  'I want my subsidiary company directors to feel that
  they are responsible for running their own business:
  but in a world of expensive money and unpredictable
  currency fluctuations I have realised that we must have
  information centrally and begin to control the finances
  from there. Last year we could have made more money
  on currency and inflation planning than some of our
  subsidiaries did on their operations. Of course, none
  of this would be feasible without our information

system. But in a world in which your competitors operate this way, you must follow.'

There is an economic imperative to develop the information system plans in line with the commercial realities of the way business must now be done. Nevertheless the style of management may be affected, as we saw above, and as the following company executive felt dramatically.

- 'This is the end of decentralisation as we have known it. You mark my words, from now on the autonomy we have enjoyed in the subsidiaries will be lost. Within two years the information system boys will be running this business.' This was the reaction of the Finance Director of Prime Electronics (1), the UK subsidiary of a US company, when he learned that a Vice-President, Information Systems had been appointed at the Head Office.

The impact on manpower and management strategies

The people resource is crucial to most organisations. Indeed one of the most frequent causes of failure to meet a particular strategic thrust is not shortage of markets, capacity or money but the lack of trained staff of the appropriate calibre at the right time.

- A British company, in the construction industry, operated with five distinct divisions, each with considerable autonomy. The Divisional Chief Executives were responsible for a targeted return on investment. The Head Office staff was kept quite small. Most records, including personnel records, were kept at divisional level.

  The Personnel Director at Head Office had the idea of centralising the employee files. He foresaw significant benefits and cost savings arising if employee data was available centrally as well as in each division. Firstly he could make effective group-wide plans for management development and succession. Secondly there would be cost savings from the elimination of duplication in clerical staffs. Thirdly he could undertake manpower planning exercises in line with group plans. Finally he could complete government and other statistical reports without reference to each division.

His proposals were greeted with considerable antagonism by each of the five Divisional Chief Executives. They felt that the records should be where the people were. It was explained that, with an on-line system, they could access the files for their staff immediately. They expressed concern about confidentiality and doubted the wisdom of putting judgemental data, such as suitability for promotion, on to a computer file. It was pointed out that this data was kept on the present hand-written records. But the most telling argument was the shift of authority from the Division to the Head Office. As one of the Divisional Chiefs, himself a steel erector in his early career, expressed it:

'You don't really expect me to agree, do you, when some other Chief Executive can pinch my best men, just when I've trained them and have plans for them. Let him find his own people, like I had to. I'm responsible for the bottom line in my Division: no one at Head Office is going over my head'.

Technically the centralisation of the personnel files in a company like this would have presented few problems. The implications, strategically, in the way the business was run, would have been significant. The Group Managing Director decided not to proceed with the project.

- Another British company, that did centralise their personnel records, found themselves running into a different problem. The Trade Unions demanded access to the file, as they were entitled to under collective bargaining legislation, to make comparisons between labour rates at different plants.

Although the data was, theoretically, available before from the manual records, the creation of the computer based system had made the possibility attainable. The company are now considering disbanding the centralised file.

The effect on acquisition strategies

Although the impact of information system developments on marketing, financial and manpower strategies may be obvious, the possibility of a link between acquisition strategies and computer plans may be less apparent. However strategic effects have arisen in practice.

- A factor in the ultimate failure of the Penn Central Railroad was the inability to link computer systems satisfactorily. The Pennsylvanian Railroad merged with the New York Central Railroad anticipating major savings from joint operations, and hoping to stave off the threatened failure of each line independently. But many of the expected benefits failed to materialise when the two information systems were found to be incompatible.

- When BOAC merged with BEA to form British Airways, the BEA seat reservation system had to be scrapped.

- When Pan American Airways merged with National Airlines there were technological problems in matching the two computer-based systems.

- In a British food company the benefits from scale economies of distribution, expected to arise when they acquired a large distributor of similar products, has still not been achieved. Their coding and file structures were totally incompatible.

The impact on overall strategy

In some cases the significance of the information system developments has been so great that the way the company is run has changed basically.

- During the 1950s and 1960s a major international company, in the motor industry, was organised by product and geographical divisions. Divisional Managers were profit responsible for the performance of their Division and had responsibilities for the sales of a particular product range or for vehicles in that particular country.

During the 1970s a global telecommunication and information system was developed which linked the
various Divisions together and with the Head Office
in the United States. Initially the system was used to
improve the reporting relationships between the
various parts of the organisation and the corporate
office.

However, in recent years the overall logistics of the
business have been centralised. Instead of Divisional
Managers being responsible for production planning
and control, deciding themselves what products to
make in response to their own market demands, such
decisions are now taken centrally. The production
control section in the corporate office now instructs,
via the information system, each manufacturing plant
on its production schedules.

One of the principal advantages of this approach is
that production requirements can be met in those
plants, and those locations, which have the greatest
capacity at the time. Should one facility be closed,
perhaps by industrial action on the part of its own
workers or those of its suppliers, or if it is overloaded,
production can be switched to another plant in a different location.

As the Chief Executive Officer said 'Labour stability
is becoming unpredictable right around the world.
Consequently we wanted to design an international
logistics system so that we could swap production
between locations'. There was an adverse reaction
from labour unions in the early stages of the system
development, particularly in Northern European
countries. Governments in other countries expressed
fears about this wielding of power by an 'unaccount-
able' multinational, and about the 'exporting of jobs'.
More recently the company has faced difficulties
in transmitting data across the borders of various
countries for similar reasons. (We shall discuss transborder data flows later.)

It should not be concluded, however, that the development of computer and telecommunication systems on a global basis automatically results in a shift towards centralisation of executive authority. The information system is neutral, and can be equally a force for permitting greater autonomy in the field.

- A large international organisation, in the food and beverage industry, recognised that, as developing nations expected more control over the affairs of companies resident in their midst, it was necessary to devolve authority for decision making away from the London Head Office, where it had existed for well over 100 years, towards local executive teams. This was facilitated by the development of computer based information systems which enabled the local executive group to be fully aware of the Head Office expectations whilst achieving sufficient autonomy to make local decisions.

Other important strategic questions can arise.

- Many banks in the United States of America are in the process of introducing automated teller machines. Located at bank branches, in supermarkets and at airports, the customer can deal with his bank at any time. By using a plastic card and keying in an identification number the customer can complete most routine banking transactions.

  However, under US law, banks may only operate within a given State. In some States, even, banks may only have one branch. But is an automated teller machine a branch? Could the large US banks spread a network of teller machines around the country, thereby competing with the hundreds of State banks?

  Other questions were raised by consumer groups and lobbyists concerned with potential threats to civil liberties. They recognised that the system would be collecting information about an individual. By centralising the files, and enabling them to be machine accessible, it might be easy to impose on personal privacy. For example, a profile of an individual's financial standing and consumption could be prepared—his membership of clubs, travel expenditure, consumption habits, donations to political and other causes, and so on. Or a list of contributors to a specific cause could be prepared by analysing data by payee. Would such information be permanently protected from incursion by Federal or State legislators?

In Britain, despite repeated assurances from government that data collected for one purpose would never be used for another, access to the motor vehicle licence records has been provided to investigators wanting to compare social security payment records.

- In Canada, a debt collection and credit agency recognised that its whole market future was at risk as banks considered introducing electronic funds transfer systems. If banks co-ordinated a network of customer accounts, all the information that the credit agency supplied to its customers, enquiring about the credit worthiness of a particular person, would be available in the bank's system and they could offer a quicker and guaranteed information service to the credit agency's customers. The potential impact on their strategy was fundamental.

Finally, consider the strategic significance of this example;-*

- A large organisation, operating throughout the United Kingdom, faced a difficult decision. They planned to introduce a major, computer-based system that would handle a large part of their paperwork throughout the country. Discussions were held with potential suppliers and highly competitive quotations were obtained. Which equipment should they choose?

* The information in this brief case history has been obtained from newspaper reports. Although the official record will show a much more detailed and involved process, the essential message that computer-based systems and organisational strategy and structure are inevitably entwined, is irrefutable.

The computer strategy recommended by the organisation's experts was for a country-wide network based on computers in twelve regional centres. Each of the 600 local offices would be linked to the system and to each other through thousands of video terminals. It was hoped, after a year's proving trial in one region, the system could be implemented within two years.

When the decision finally came before the decision-makers the recommendation from the experts was over-ruled. No single computer manufacturer seemed able to meet all of the criteria thought important by the board members. Moreover, they wondered if the rapid advance in technology might produce a better way of automating the organisation's work other than through regional computer centres.

In the end the board referred the problem back to the experts, suggesting that they look for an alternative solution. Basically they wondered whether a compromise could be found which would not make them dependent on any one manufacturer. They also asked whether it would be possible to replace the regional networks with clusters of smaller machines able to operate independently as well as being linked to the country-wide network.

The system experts recognised that the rejection of their proposals was tantamount to a reversal of the basic computer strategy. Ironically they had considered a distributed processing network in the early stages of their study and rejected it because it would have meant a fundamental change in the way in which the organisation did its work.

It is not unusual to find that a computer system strategy, conceived as an operational support to the activities of the enterprise, proves to have the most significant organisational implication and to affect the overall, long term strategies of the organisation. In fact the case just described is the British Inland Revenue and their proposals to computerise the entire Pay As You Earn income tax system. It was the British Cabinet that rejected the experts' proposals, which took nearly three years of detailed planning, and demanded a new study of alternative ways to computerise PAYE.

The potential for catastrophe

- 'We suddenly became aware that the entire business was dependent on that computer . . .
  President of a New York Corporation

The computing and telecommunication systems of many companies today are so fundamental to their work, and failure so potentially catastrophic that we must devote an entire chapter (9) to the matter. In the context of our present thinking, however, we must recognise how vulnerable the modern organisation can become through its dependence on its information systems. To take a few examples by way of illustration:-

- It is now impossible to load the modern jumbo aircraft by manual means. If the computers go off the air, the plane will not fly.

- In a bank with centralised customer accounts, as in the major British clearing banks, if the system goes down for any period, not only can no transactions be recorded but the bank no longer knows what funds it has in the system. It cannot survive for long in this condition.

- An American furniture company lost its computer records in a fire. Unable to recreate the files it advertised for its customers to send in what was owing. There were no replies. The company no longer exists.

- The Wells Fargo Bank of San Francisco lost a reported $21 million in a computer fraud involving the manipulation of money between accounts.

Such contingencies can be guarded against, at a price; as we shall see in chapter 9. But before that can happen senior management have to recognise the strategic significance of their information systems.

The Information Systems Strategy

These case examples have all been taken from real life: they are not academic abstractions. Information systems can have a major strategic impact. System developments can no longer be treated as purely technical or operational matters. Information systems have moved beyond providing support to the rest of the enterprise; increasingly they are its core. Their effect in marketing, financial, production, acquisition and other strategic endeavours is great; as are their implications for new organisation structures and the way management operates. So, too, is the threat of calamity.

Senior management must think through its information systems strategy in the context of the overall corporate strategy. How it may do so will be described in chapter 7. For the first time management can move beyond reactive management to create an organisation with the structure and style it wants. But it has to know what it wants!

Let us move ahead by considering the importance of information in the modern organisation. This is where much confusion about managing information in the modern organisation arises.

Reference

1. The detailed case study of Prime Electronics is contained in: Tricker, R. I. and R. Boland: *Management Information and Control Systems* (2nd edition): Wiley; 1981.

2
The Importance of Information

•*what information really is and why data is a crucial resource*

'I have the finest executive team, better information systems and far more reports than my predecessors ever had: yet I feel less in command of the situation, less aware of what's really going on than they ever were.'

> *The Chairman of a major British public company*

'We suffer from paralysis by analysis.'

> *Executive in a Canadian company*

The Need for Information

• Long ago, in ancient Egypt, the Pharaoh was working on his pyramid project.

'Never before, in the history of man', he remarked, 'has the world known the wonders that our generation is seeing. We live in a world of change. I face complexities, uncertainties and risks unknown to my predecessors. What I need is information and', he added, 'all they give me are reports.'

Decision makers have always sought information. Modern executive, medieval farmer and ancient Pharaoh alike need to be informed. Whether launching a new product, ploughing the fields or building a pyramid they want information about the state of their resources and knowledge about the uncertain future events they may have to face. Decision making is an information process.

But though the need for information does not change, situations do. By modern standards the Pharaoh's world was relatively straightforward; he also exercised total power over his slave employees. His counterpart today exists in a vastly complex world in which information is the basis of significant power. The process of management has changed over the centuries. Since we seek to understand the management of information in the modern organisation, these are ideas we must explore further.

Moreover the means of providing information have changed. The Pharaoh could be driven in his chariot around his pyramid in a matter of moments. His information came from direct observation and first hand reports from his overseers. The executive today receives messages from a multiplicity of sources, through a wide range of media. He can access data-bases, call on vast stores of accumulated knowledge, send and receive messages by satellite instantaneously around the globe. But the potential bombardment by data does not, necessarily, result in him being better informed than his predecessors. We shall need to understand the nature of information if we are to manage it professionally in the modern enterprise.

In this chapter, therefore, let us see how ideas about information have evolved, why data is modern manager's resource, what information is and why it is so pertinent to organisation, and finally, how information is a basis of power in the modern world.

A New Interest in Information

Surprisingly the idea of information did not excite the early management writers. The classical works focus on the functions of management—planning, controlling, co-ordinating, organising and leadership. Information is not mentioned. Like sunlight to the Victorian botanist, clearly it was crucial to the process, but either it was available, or it was not. Without it there was little to be done.

Subsequent writers, of the behavioural and human relations schools of thought, recognised that management involved achieving results through people. They were certainly concerned about communication. But, again, the notion of information was not developed.

Only in the later years of the 20th century has attention focused on information itself. Contributors to the systems view of management, whilst appreciating the classical emphasis on

the work that a manager actually does, and accepting the behavioural recognition that management involves people, both
individually and in groups, fundamentally focus on management
as the process of making and taking decisions. Management involves information. Consequently information is a vital aspect
of management.

Some commentators assume that the main reason for this
new found interest in information was the development of computer and telecommunications technology. With the technical
ability to capture, transmit, store, process and retrieve masses
of text and data globally they argue it was now worthwhile
thinking about managers' information needs. But this is only
part of the story. The dominant reason for the new found interest
in information lies not in technology but in changes that have
occurred in the managerial situation and the management response to them.

From Responding to Causing Change

The managerial situation throughout the Western world in
the past ten or fifteen years, and particularly since the mid 70s,
has been typified by various changes, each of which has significantly affected the need for information. Consider some of them:

Increasing scale, concentration and diversity

Organisationally and financially enterprises are tending to
become larger and more interconnected. Internal growth and
strategies of growth by acquisition (accompanied by policies of
realistic divestment) have both contributed to increasing corporate scale.

In many mature markets—aircraft, automobiles, chemicals
and large computers, for example— fewer, larger firms compete
world wide. Joint ventures and other associations between companies, often with government support, have become necessary
to procure the funds essential to research, develop and launch
a new product or build a new, high-technology production
facility. Examples abound—British Leyland links with Honda;
UK government backing for the De Lorean car in Northern
Ireland; and in the aircraft field—Concorde, the European Air-
Bus and most military aircraft today involve joint ventures.

Markets for products and services become increasingly international. The Ford 'world car' and IBM's equipment available internationally are but two examples. The provision of financial services, and the operation of financial markets, have also become internationally interdependent. The take-over of US banks by British banks underlines this move.

But contrariwise, whilst markets become more concentrated, companies are also becoming more diverse. Avoiding dependency on one market place or product range, shifting from decaying lines of business and the spreading of risk is leading firms into diverse and different activities. Tobacco companies develop food, drink and leisure industry divisions. Oil companies move into coal, atomic power, metals, animal nutrition, even retailing.

- AT & T, the Bell Telephone system in America, for a hundred years the epitome of service providing telephones throughout the United States, has repositioned itself to emphasise profitable, competitive growth through business computing and telecommunications and with home electronics. They realise that this is the era of information.

Increasing scale, concentration and diversity, accompanied by the internationalisation of business, leads to new organisational structures and entirely different calls for information. Systems developed to facilitate information and control in less complex situations frequently fail to meet the needs of the new structure.

A diagram of communication and data channels in a modern organisation (which might have autonomous divisions, wholly and partly owned subsidiaries, central corporate services, global business streams mapped across regional entities, joint ventures, associated businesses, task forces and project groups) is more likely to resemble a plate of spaghetti than a neat organisational pyramid. But such is the decision making reality of the modern enterprise. Information needs emerge and change continuously as the transient structure adapts to changing situations.

Nor is this position unique to the private sector. Similar trends toward scale, concentration and diversity can be detected in nationalised industries and public utilities, police forces and the military, education and health care, and in local and national government sectors.

How different from the world of the classical entrepreneur.

Greater complexity in decisions

The entrepreneur is enshrined in the mythology of management, for his supposed freedom to act decisively and ability to take risks. The entrepreneurial greats gave their name to the companies they founded--and in some cases nearly destroyed as they failed to adapt—Alfred Herbert, Henry Ford, Dupont, Morris, Woolworth. Nor is the breed extinct: Laker, Tiny Rowlands of Lonhro and Maxwell of Pergamon Press exhibit the same abilities.

The world view of the entrepreneur is relatively simple. It has to be. He handles the principal information channels himself. A hallmark of the entrepreneur is that he is at the heart of his enterprise. His image is stamped throughout. He knows his people, visits his domain and is personally involved in the operations.

Moreover he is personally in touch with the business environment. It is he who makes the key deals with the customers, negotiates with the bankers, argues with the suppliers and watches the competition. A mental sketchmap of the entrepreneur might cover:-

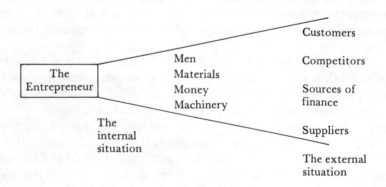

Figure 2/1

Faced with a crucial decision—to change the basic technology, acquire another company, open a new facility, alter the gearing, change the organisation—he can marshall the facts he needs himself. He knows that this is his, unique, task. Not for him the complex, bureaucratic information systems of accountants and system experts: the true entrepreneur is his own information system through personal involvement.

By contrast, the modern executive facing any such strategic decisions would feel that it was necessary to monitor a host of sources of potential information. He knows that the economic, political, social, international and technological circumstances can all affect, significantly, the outcome of his plans. Consequently his 'world view', his mental map has wider boundaries, is more flexible and transient, and is infinitely more complex than that of the entrepreneur. (*see figure 2/2*)

As a result the modern executive has the need of support from a variety of information systems. He cannot monitor the complex situation on his own.

He also has to decide what information he needs. This is far more difficult than it appears on the surface. It represents a new, and crucial, management task. In earlier centuries only the scholar faced this problem. The rest of the people could respond intuitively to the world as they saw it—to whatever messages came their way. Until recently this was the approach of the manager. The dawn of scientific thought added the scientist to those who had to determine what information they needed. Now it is the turn of the manager to identify, understand and determine his information needs.

Figure 2/2 also indicates how entities, which traditionally were thought to be 'external to the business', are increasingly making information demands on it.

Increasing external demands for information

Corporations, particularly large ones, are seen now to exercise significant power by various groups in society who believe their legitimate rights are affected and, thus, that there is a need for regulation. And regulation necessitates information. A few examples will show how widespread is the call on companies for information and accountability.

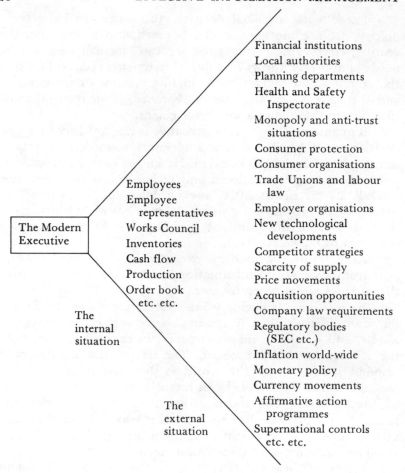

Figure 2/2

In pursuit of economic, social and political policies governmental regulatory demands come not only from local and national governments but from supernational bodies such as the European Community for operations in member states, or the United Nations for multinational operations. Demands can also be international, such as the EEC code of practice (1) or the Sullivan code for US companies operating in South Africa.

The consumer movement, particularly in the United States where the legal doctrine of class actions and contingent fees

encourages litigation, has put demands, both legal and exhorta-
tory, on companies for greater disclosure. Whilst in Europe the
emphasis on industrial democracy, with its various degrees from
rights of access to information, through types of involvement
and participation, to codetermination in decision-making, has
emphasised employee demands for information.

> As Lord Bullock writes in his committee report (2)
> on industrial democracy in Britain—'eventually we
> have to decide whether access to information should
> be given ex-gratia by employers or demanded as a
> right by employees'. It depends, of course, whether
> one sees the company as an outgrowth of capitalism
> with the prerogative to manage lying with shareholder
> and management; or whether one perceives the modern
> corporation as a partnership between capital and
> labour.

Expectations of the corporation, from institutional in-
vestors, consumers, employees and society at large (represented
by many interest groups) do seem to be changing. Intuition and
'feel' about companies are giving way to enquiry and analysis.
Consequently there is call for wider documentation and disclosure. Accountability for and the legitimacy of specific actions
are questioned.

> The Corporate Report (3) produced by the UK ac-
> counting bodies, proposed that every economic entity,
> which by its actions could affect the interests of others,
> should be called on to report on its activities to such
> interest groups. Not surprisingly these proposals pro-
> voked considerable hostility, because they expose the
> nerve ends of a society in which information is a basis
> of power.

In France, following the Sudreau report, companies are
now required to publish a social report along with their annual
accounts, which details company policies and activities in fields
such as labour, consumers and ecology. In the United States the
10K Form, required by the Securities and Exchange Commission
(SEC) supplements the published annual report and accounts
with major amounts of data on past performance and future
plans.

In the public sector, too, there is a demand for more openness in government and greater disclosure of information. The enactment of the Freedom of Information Act in the United States, which enables those with legitimate interests widespread access to government files, is an example of the trend; so is the wider use of referenda and city meetings that is found in Canadian communities. In Europe the tussle between executive privilege to confidentiality and interest group demands for access to information and openness is still in its infancy.

Compared with the situation of fifteen or twenty years ago, however, it can justifiably be claimed that the modern organisation is under pressure to be more visible, its operations more apparent, its walls thinner and more transparent, than ever before.

Turbulence, ambiguity and the management of change

Whereas the world of the manager was relatively secure until a decade or two ago, his information straight-forward, his situation relatively clear and his prerogative to manage unassailed, today the decision-maker faces a world of continuous turbulence.

The rate of change seems to accelerate. In so many fields of human endeavour—energy consumption, agricultural production, speed of travel, population, effects of weaponry—this acceleration can be seen. It is graphically charted in the Toffleresque curve of figure 2/3.

Such turbulence and change make big demands for information. The greater the uncertainty, the greater the need for information; and the more valuable the information that really reduces that uncertainty.

The dilemma for the modern manager is coping with ambiguity in his decision-making. Despite the feasibility of receiving reports by video-screen and print-out, despite the ability to access masses of data, more than ever before, he has to cope with greater complexity, more unknowns and wider uncertainty than ever.

Management, which used to involve overcoming the problems brought about by changing circumstances to get back on track towards the corporate objective, today has become the process of causing change.

Information, the basis of decision-making power, has become managements' principal need; and managing the data resource their most crucial activity.

But before we continue our exploration of the professional management of information we should pause. What *is* information? How does it differ from data? Are we really clear what we have in mind?

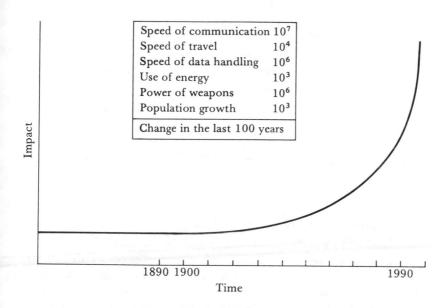

Change in the last 100 years	
Speed of communication	10^7
Speed of travel	10^4
Speed of data handling	10^6
Use of energy	10^3
Power of weapons	10^6
Population growth	10^3

Figure 2/3

The Nature of Information

There has been a lack of clarity in thinking about information. It is an ambiguous and potentially deceptive concept. Surprisingly the management theorist has little to tell us. Information can be considered at various levels.

— Level one : basic data

At the most basic level we can recognise a record of a primary transaction or situation. The height, weight and age of a person; the date, amount and payee of a cheque; or the product group, quantity produced and shift number, for examples. These are the primary reflection of fundamental processes or states. 'Raw data' is what they are frequently called. Raw, or basic data are the building blocks which contain the potential information: but only after processing.

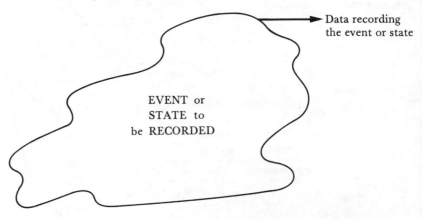

Figure 2/4

—— *Level two : information as message*

Basic data is frequently aggregated and analysed. Personal characteristics become details of a class; cheques drawn are totalled to show the effect on cash flow; production statistics emerge from the elements in production records.

Now such data is made available in a report, a book, pictures on a screen or an announcement from a loud-speaker, for example. Many people think of this as information. The information is the message.

No concern is given to the needs of the recipient of the message, nor to any meaning he derives from it. Information, at this level, is seen as a function of the message alone. Information and data are synonymous for such a view.

For our purposes it will be more useful to call these basic messages 'data'; and to retain the idea of information for use when the potential user of the message is identified.

Clearly more data, more readily available does not lead to better informed executives. Stories of computer print-outs unused by the managers for whom they were prepared are legion. Many so-called information systems in the past concentrated on the handling of data—ignoring the real information needs of the potential user.

Some accounting systems, too, fail to identify the user's needs adequately, particularly those which result in complex financial reports intended to provide standard information for a multitude of users. The preparer of the report (the sender, in fig. 2/5) has determined the content with inadequate concern for the user's perception of his information needs.

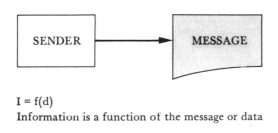

I = f(d)
Information is a function of the message or data

Figure 2/5

Shannon (4), in the communication theory he developed, used a mathematical measure of probability to quantify the properties of specific symbols to convey messages. He identified three levels of information:

A — the technical level concerned with how accurately symbols can be transmitted

B — the semantic level concerned with how precisely do symbols convey meaning

C — the effectiveness level concerned with how effectively docs the meaning derived affect conduct.

Shannon's work concentrated on level A and has important uses for the telecommunications engineer. The student of management information, however, is concerned primarily with the final level. But the idea of probability, which Shannon introduced, is valuable as we shall see.

— — Level three : information in use

In reality information involves the receiver of the message; it is data that has been interpreted. The user is essential for information to acquire a value; before that it is data. Consequently information involves a process—a human thought process. It is dynamic: it is not an entity. As Henry Boettinger puts it— 'information has no meaning unless its final destination is in the cerebral cortex'.

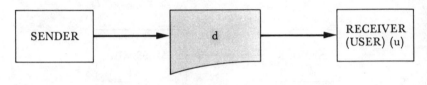

$I = f(d, u)$
Information involves the message and the user

Figure 2/6

The user (u) is involved in this definition of information. His ability to receive the data and deduce some meaning becomes important. The sender must now be aware of language, semantics and symbols that are relevant to the recipient.

Obviously an identical message can have different meanings for different people. Intelligence, education, training in the language or notation used in the data, previous relevant experience and perceptual abilities can all affect the meaning derived from the data.

● The message that the patient's temperature is 104 degrees is likely to have a different meaning to the patient, his doctor and his accountant.

Information, viewed in this context, becomes an idiosyncratic process involving differing human beings. It also takes us closer to an understanding of information that will be useful in improving information management in the modern organisation.

Level four : valuable information

If we are to appreciate the concept of information in its totality we must be concerned with the meaning the user actually derives from the source data. We are interested in the extent to which his uncertainty is reduced and his knowledge increased.

Not only must we recognise the user, but appreciate his organisational role. We need to understand the role he perceives himself playing; recognise that his expectations are important.

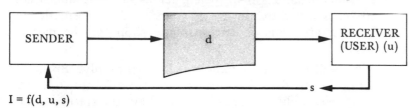

$I = f(d, u, s)$

Information is a function of

- Message
- User
- User's organisational situation

Figure 2 / 7

At this high level information is a function of the data, the user and the user's situation. A person can receive different information from identical messages if his role in perceiving them differs. For example, the simple message that taxes are to be raised to pay an increased salary to teachers will have different information content for an individual when he thinks as a tax payer, a school teacher, or a prospective candidate for political office.

> Peter Drucker tells a pertinent story. A visitor to a building site saw three stone masons, each apparently working on similar pieces of stone. He asked the first what he was doing.
> 'Carving this stone', he replied.
> He asked the second.
> 'I am making the lintel for a door', he said.
> But the third replied:
> 'I am building a cathedral'.

By including the message (data d), the recipient (user u) and the user's situation (s) in our model of information it is apparent that organisation structure, management development and organisational development are closely related to the study of management information systems.

Data has a cost : information a value

Another way of thinking about information emphasises, again, that it acquires its value in use.

> Consider what happens when, let us say, a financial controller is asked by the works manager for information on brass scrap metal in the machine shop for the past six weeks.
>
> 'That will be a costly exercise', he might reply. 'Six weeks is not the standard accounting period, we do not code brass scrap separately and I really do not have the staff to undertake such an exercise'.

The provider of data recognises that the cumulative cost of providing data rises. As the straight line in Fig. 2/8 suggests, each additional element of data has a marginal cost. Of course, in practice the rising cost of providing data is seldom a straight line, increasing by units as additional staff and computing facilities are added.

However, although data has the cost associated with it, information acquires value as it is useful to the user.

> The value of the scrap report to the works manager might have been quite low. If, for example, he only wanted to satisfy the request of a visiting dignatory. In which case, had the controller estimated the cost of the data, he could have said that was greater than its value to him. Or the value of the information might have been considerable. If, for example, he was thinking of retooling the entire workshop to reduce scrap significantly. Then the cost of the data would pale into insignificance beside the value of the information.

In Fig. 2/8 the value of the information to the user is shown as the curved line. When the recipient knows nothing on the subject each new element of data reduces his uncertainty considerably. Consequently it will have a high marginal value over the cost of the data. As he learns more, each new piece of data adds less to his information and the additional value over the additional cost reduces. Ultimately new data adds nothing more to his knowledge; it might even serve to confuse him.

Some accountants and systems designers treat information as though it was a free good—floating around in the air to be utilised. In reality data has a cost—a cost which is tending to

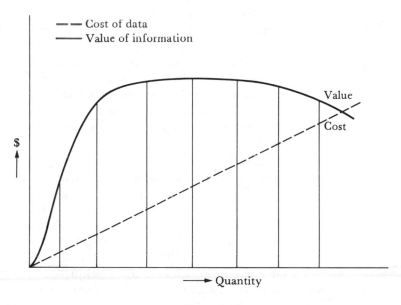

Figure 2/8

escalate in many large organisations: whereas information acquires value in use. Consequently data can be bought and sold. That is what Marshall Mcluen had in mind when he wrote 'information is the crucial commodity'. Norbert Weiner, on the other hand was thinking of level four information when he wrote 'information is what changes us. It is not a commodity to be bought and sold'.

The implications of distinguishing data and information, and of emphasising that information involves message, user and the user's decision context, are crucial to our study of information systems strategy, as we shall see.

Level of Decision

Another way of understanding information is to distinguish different needs for information at various levels of decision. The classical view of managerial decision making identifies three levels:-

Strategic	Concerned with the longer term direction of the enterprise and its interaction with the external environment. Strategic levels determine the particular mission and objectives and lay down policy guidelines for lower decision levels. e.g. The decision to make a take-over bid for another enterprise, to change the fundamental technology, to start operations in another country, to significantly alter the capital structure and so on.
Managerial	Sometimes called the technical or management control level which is fundamentally concerned with the allocation of resources and pursuit of the overall strategies. If the strategic level is concerned with 'what' the enterprise is to do, the managerial level is concerned with 'how'. e.g. To determine production schedules, the working of overtime, or to manage redundancy programmes.
Operational	Concerned with executing the managerial requirements.

At the operational level one is typically concerned with great detail within a relatively narrow framework of reference. At the managerial level the boundaries of the situation in view have broadened; whilst at the strategic level one is concerned with the interactions between the enterprise and its outside world at a relatively high level of abstraction.

The type of decision process changes too. At the operational level many of the decisions are essentially programmable. That is, rules can be determined for the effective decision process. At higher levels imagination and creativity are required. The strategic decision is essentially a creative act.

Time horizons change significantly too. At the operational level decisions typically have a short time horizon, at the managerial level the decision maker is looking ahead a week or two, whilst at the strategic level the time horizon of a strategic choice may very well be years or even decades.

Operational decisions are taken in a relatively certain world. By contrast strategic decision makers face a world of considerable uncertainty. The challenge is to identify the uncertain future events which are likely to affect the outcome of the decision. The amount at risk also increases as the decision hierarchy is climbed.

Koestler (5) casts an interesting light on the creative aspect of information. He differentiates two types of thinking—the mundane and routine thought which is all on one self-consistent plane; and the creative act which always operates on more than one plane. Bringing together two self-consistent but usually incompatible 'frames of reference' creates new insights and therefore new information. 'This creative act, by connecting previously unrelated dimensions of experience, enables one to attain a higher level of mental evolution. It is an act of liberation—the defeat of habit by originality.'

Koestler goes on to suggest that this creative process, the result of the interaction between the habitually incompatible 'frames of reference' is at the root of scientific discovery, humour and artistic creation. What he does not say explicitly but which is of immediate relevance to us, is that his model is at the same time a brilliant model of the information process.

It captures what might be called the 'aha' effect—that strange, imaginative and uniquely human process by which an individual can associate two or more apparently unrelated messages. For example, something one reads in the Financial Times combined with something half remembered that a colleague has said or a chance comment at a past symposium, and suddenly there is an 'aha' that suggests a new way of looking at a situation, a new insight into the problem, a new opportunity to be explored. Information of a high order or originality and value has been created.

Efforts so far in developing information systems have tended to concentrate on single planes. We shall see opportunities in creating personal information systems which may facilitate the 'aha' factor.

Information—a basis of power

Before leaving this review of the nature of information we should recognise that information is fundamental to the exercise of power.

In primitive societies the tribal leaders, witch doctors, and priests hold the accumulated wisdom of the culture; and pass it on, with due ceremony and great care, to their successors. Their superior knowledge is a basis of their power.

So it has been through the centuries. Today insurgents seize the local television station and airport before they occupy the government buildings or the royal palace. Communication has become vital, as well, in the modern complex and inter-dependent society.

Throughout Western Europe, in recent years, managerial inclination as well as legislation has been swinging toward giving greater involvement in decisions to non-managerial employees. Differing significantly in both concept and detail between countries, the trends toward greater disclosure, participation and, in some cases, codetermination are unmistakable.

The power once vested almost exclusively in the ownership equity as the root of managerial authority, is being eroded as importance is attached to property in men's jobs and their right to be involved in decisions that might affect them.

Disclosure, an unhappy term with its unspoken implication that there are things buried, waiting to be exposed, has become a crucial topic in this debate. No longer content with published financial accounts, even if presented with pictorial pie-diagrams describing the basic facts, labour wants information about re-sources and results, prices and profits, manning and investment intentions, by company, by product and by plant. Information is fundamental. Nor has disclosure assumed this significance be-cause little more data might facilitate wage bargaining: it is because in a modern society information is not merely incidental to the exercise of power but is itself a basic source of power.

The demand for knowledge about and involvement in managerial decisions is not limited to employees and their union representatives. Consumer groups, customers, supply organisa-tions, special interest groups both locally and nationally, financial interests, local and national government administration—all, increasingly, seek a right to be involved. Such developments are occurring throughout the Western world.

Power, Mary Parker Follet observed, is the ability to make things happen. This definition of power neatly covers two different aspects:-

1.   Power 'over' people. The classic case would involve a threat of coercion. Here people are subjected to power when they do B instead of A, which they would have done had A not been loaded with deterring costs, such as punishment, penalty or non-reward.

2.   Power 'with' people. This case covers the ability to set goals, make plans and achieve objectives with others, committing them without the threat of a sanction. The power thus exercised does not involve penalties or non-reward, but the ability to control the way the other people interpret messages available to them, perceive their world and apprehend their situation. Hence a source of power lies in controlling access to and presentation of data.

Moses, leading the Children of Israel out of Egypt, had almost no power over the people but immense power with them. The kinds of organisation in which we tend to be involved today demand and depend upon high levels of information for setting goals and making strategies and plans. Consequently, power resides in the capacity to deprive people of information that would give rise to challenge or criticism, as well as to determine access to information that would encourage or commit others to act in accordance with certain strategies.

Lacking most of the sanctions open to the 19th century entrepreneur—through pricing and unbridled competition, through uninhibited plant closure or relocation, through untrammelled technological change, through penalisation or terminating the employment of labour—the late 20th century executive is faced by a barrage of competing and conflicting demands on the enterprise. Not surprisingly there has been talk of a crisis of authority and the need for a new legitimacy of enterprise. Given a widening incongruence between the expectations of participants in a business and their observations of the reality, executives will feel, as Weber suggested, the need for a wider acceptance by all participants of each other's roles and authority. In the process, politicizing of the management function becomes inevitable. Without a unifying ideology vested interest groups prosper.

No wonder that information has assumed such critical significance. Those with access to information, and particularly those involved in its communication and supply, can be on the cutting edge of social change. No longer is information the apparently free good available to economic man.

> Touraine (6), a French sociologist, saw this point: 'The principal opposition between . . . classes does not result from the fact that one possesses wealth and property and the other does not. It comes about because the dominant classes dispose of knowledge and control information'.

Information—a hallmark of evolution

The spoken and the written word—language—is unique to man. It is his greatest creation. It conveys his myths, expresses his songs and perpetuates his culture. It enables him to remember his past, record his present and imagine his future. Through language he communicates and can integrate with others. Through language, too, he can differentiate from others and perceive himself.

Lesser animals communicate visually and by the simplest vocabulary of sounds. The ability to use language represented an enormous evolutionary step for man. The information content of language is fundamental to the process of being human, to the creation of organisation and to the viability of a society.

The evolution of species is marked by increasing complexity, greater interconnectedness and higher levels of information. In recent years man's rapidly growing ability to capture, store, transmit and retrieve data offers the potential for higher orders of human relationship between individuals, organisations and societies: but the opportunity has first to be recognised.

Managing the data resource becomes a critical activity, if the information potential is to be realised. In the management world of the '60s and '70s—the first two decades of computing—it became well accepted that top management involvement was necessary. But usually that meant appointing effective professionals to direct operational level system developments. Today that is not enough.

In the modern organisation information systems and organisation are intertwined. There are pressures on organisations to change more quickly than information systems can adapt. Increasingly the information system is not just a transaction processing system developed to support the operations of the enterprise: it is at the *core* of the organisation, an essential part of the key activities. Increasingly the organisation is dependent on its information systems. The potential for crisis, even catastrophe, is significant; so is the opportunity for increased efficiency and effectiveness.

Modern management stands on the threshold of a vast new array of issues, threats and opportunities. In the following chapters we will consider how professional management can pursue them.

References

1. *Code of Conduct for companies with interests in South Africa.* Adopted by Nine Member States of the European Community 20 September 1977. UK Government Guidance, Cmnd. 7233.
2. *The Bullock Report.* Report of the Committee of Inquiry on Industrial Democracy. Chairman, Lord Bullock. January 1977. Cmnd. 6706.
3. *The Corporate Report.* A discussion paper published by the Accounting Standards Steering Committee. London 1975.
4. Shannon, C. and W. Weaver; *Mathematical theory of communication;* University of Illinois, 1959.
5. Koestler, Arthur; *The Act of Creation;* Hutchinson & Co., 1964, Pan Books 1975.
6. Touraine, A.; *The Post Industrial Society; Random House,* 1971 (tr. Mayhew), Wildwood House, London, 1974.

3
Rethinking the Systems Organisation
•roles for users and experts: a new way of looking at MIS

'I am the Director of Information Systems. Our annual expenditure is close to £100 million on systems. Yet I am not technically competent in any of the relevant spheres of expertise.'
Director (I.S.) in a large company, London, England.

'Why should the Finance VP be entirely responsible for computing? He only uses a fraction of the data.'
Information Systems Manager, Winnipeg, Canada.

'The VP Information Systems and the Controller are in constant battle. When the last CEO left, the Information Systems VP went too: you have to have a friend at court.'
Senior executive, Washington, USA.

An Evolution in Information System Organisation

Seven ages of IS

Initially it was straightforward. When 'hands-on' experience of computers meant knowing the trauma of dropping a tray of punched cards on the way from the sorter, identifying the responsibility for systems was simple. Today with networks of equipment enabling access to files from screens throughout the organisation and processing capabilities from terminals in different divisions and sections of the business it is less clear. Yet this is the starting point for understanding the effective management of information in the modern enterprise. Let us trace the changes that have occurred, remembering that only a few organisations are on the frontier. Most are still somewhere back along the track.

1.   *The early days.*   Initially the application of computers in business tended to replace existing manual records and clerical tasks- payroll, inventory records, billing/invoicing, cost records, ledger work. Since these activities were in the accounts department, what could be more natural than placing the responsibility for system development and managing the computer department under the accountant. Often it was his boss, the Finance Director, who had initiated the use of computers anyway.

As long as each application was a discrete entity and the inputs and outputs remained within the accounting function there were few organisational issues. Computers were an adjunct to the accounts department.

THE EARLY STAGES

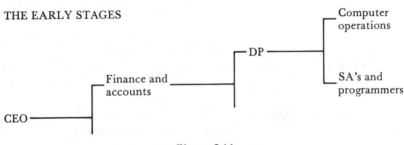

Figure 3 / 1

2.   *User involvement.*   However applications began to straddle organisational boundaries. For example, an order-entry system took its inputs from the sales department, and was widely used by them; but it also provided the data to drive the despatch system, which in turn provided inputs to the billing/invoicing routine—and so on. The responsibility for inputs and the interest in the outputs no longer resided in the accounting department alone.

The usual solution to this organisational dilemma was to leave the full responsibility for computing within the accounts department, but to create teams to develop the application systems with members drawn from those departments concerned to work with the systems analysts and programmers.

It was often at this stage that problems of direction and control in computing began to occur.

Richard Nolan (1) has developed a well known analysis of the typical stages through which companies go in their management of the computer and data processing resource. His experience has lead him to identify:

Stage 1—Initiation	in which there is enthusiasm.
Stage 2—Contagion	systems developments and computing really take off; functional boundaries in the organisation are crossed. Much enthusiasm leads to high and rising costs. Crises occur.
Stage 3—Control	top management, concerned at the crises as expenditure rises and systems fail to meet expectations or timing, take firm control. Budgets and project controls are imposed. The organisational responsibilities for DP are clarified.
Stage 4—Integration	and maturity of system efforts and the professional management of DP and computers.
Subsequent stages—	further developments as data-base is introduced and growing maturity and dependence on DP in the company.

Nolan's progression is much rooted in the evolution of computer equipment through successive generations, but has been, nevertheless, a helpful tool of managerial diagnosis.

The literature of computing is littered with horrific tales of computer failure. In a catalogue of causes written back in 1968, McKinsey pinpointed the lack of top management involvement as a key reason for failure to develop systems on time, within budget and to meet the operating criteria.

The formation of top management computer steering committees and data-processing policy groups was the typical response. The cross-functional issues and the longer term aspects were resolved at this level, although functional responsibility for computing remained with the finance and accounting function. We will consider the top management role in the development of an information systems strategy in chapter 7.

USER INVOLVEMENT

Figure 3/2

3. *The separation of functions.* Once computing became widely adopted within an organisation, the proportion of time and data storage devoted to accountancy work fell. Often it was only a small percentage of the whole. The original rationale for putting the DP function under accounting no longer applied.

But, predictably, a power struggle ensued for any who would wrest the responsibility from the accounts and controllership function. On their side it was argued by the accountants that they now had the expertise, that the installation was being professionally and efficiently run, that the joint development teams met user problems and that the controllership function was now developing to embrace an information function.

The counter arguments reported the problems of conflicts of interest, failures to produce reports on time, errors, and system breakdowns. More penetratingly they voiced the fear that the Controller cast himself in the role of corporate watchdog, policing the activities of other departments, and consequently was an inappropriate person to control corporate information services.

In some organisations at this stage the responsibility for computers and data-processing is shifted out of the finance and

SEPARATION OF FUNCTIONS

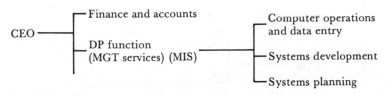

Figure 3/3

accounting bailiwick. A separate DP function is created. In practice this often follows a major crisis or internal reorganisation and power shuffle. In some cases it is facilitated by the existence of a management services function that can assume the responsibility. In many cases, though, the responsibility still resides under the finance and accounting arm of the organisation.

4.   *Professional DP management.* We can now focus on the organisation and management of the DP function (as it was typically called although Information Systems Dept. and Computing Dept. were common).

In many larger enterprises DP was now the employer of hundreds of staff members and the consumer of millions in annual budget—up to 1% or more of annual revenues was not unusual. Various distinctive tasks within DP are differentiated by this stage.

Day to day operation of the computer mainframes and central data storage and peripheral devices has become a production activity. Tight managerial controls, with an emphasis on efficiency and productivity, are feasible. The data centre (or 'shop' as it is colloquially known in the DP profession), has become a production operation.

Systems development, on the other hand, has become more specialised: more related to the business reality and less constrained by the inward-looking requirements of programming and computers. Because it is a creative, imaginative process, involving users and system experts, open-ended project controls are more appropriate than tight budgetary controls. Resources of man-hours and facilities are budgeted, over a given time horizon, to achieve specific system objectives. Now the validation is on cost-effectiveness, relating system costs with anticipated benefits.

An example of the grouping in a DP function at this stage might include:-

PROFESSIONAL DP MANAGEMENT

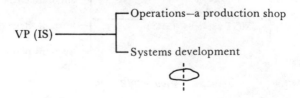

5. *Data administration.*   The separation of systems development activities from computer operations is intuitively obvious— it is analogous to the separation between product development and production. The next stage, however, is less apparent.

In large computer-assisted systems, particularly those with major data bases, it becomes appropriate to identify clearly the responsibility for data administration. This function is charged with the task of setting and maintaining standards and procedures in the use of the data base, of creating and developing a data dictionary to enable items of data to be uniformly filed and retrieved, and of ensuring the integrity—that is the accuracy, relevance, completeness and honesty—of the data. As we shall see, in chapter 5, when data is held corporately for the use of different departments, functions, subsidiaries or divisions, it is imperative that it is reliable. This is the duty of data administration.

An additional responsibility has been added more recently of running an information centre. This is a facility to bridge the potential gap between user, with information needs, and the data available. The staff need to be user orientated, to understand the user's needs, but knowledgeable in the content and process of the data files. Again, this will be explored further in chapter 5 which considers the management of management's crucial resource—data.

At this stage the IS organisation might look like this:-

DATA ADMINISTRATION

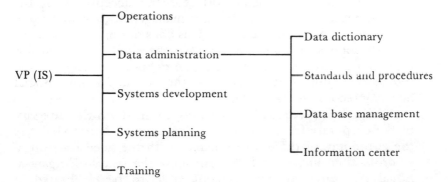

6. *The user becomes king.* The great breakthrough in the development of information systems which really has an impact occurs when the user ceases to think of the system and the data as 'theirs' and openly speaks of 'our system' and 'my data'. Having been commended by computer manufacturers and business school professors for over a decade, more and more companies in practice are organising to swing the dominant emphasis in systems work onto the user.

Now the organisational schema might look like:-

USER IS KING

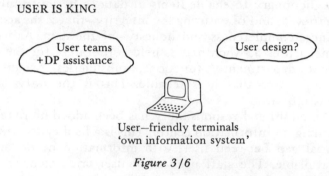

User—friendly terminals
'own information system'

Figure 3/6

This user orientation in systems, as we shall see in more detail later, has been facilitated by the use of terminals that are 'user friendly' in accessing data that are relevant to their needs. Now the potential user can take command of his situation. He can determine his information needs, initiate the necessary system development, participate in the system building and be held responsible for 'signing-off' for the acceptance of the system. Systems teams can be user managed with systems personnel acting as DP consultants. This does not mean, of course, that all applications will be like this: there will also be major, transaction based systems in their own right—for example a payroll system, billing procedures, or the British National Social Security records in Newcastle.

Now the questions become how to maintain the integrity of the corporate files, how to exercise control, how to balance the autonomy of the decision maker with the need for central co-ordination and control. We can sense the issues of organisational structure and management style to be elaborated in chapter 6.

7. *A corporate communications function.* A further separation of function occurs when organisations progress far along the road of telecommunications and computing. Interests in office automation—text editing, word processing, facsimile, conferencing, executive work stations and other ideas we will consider in the next chapter—serve to accelerate this development.

The extent of the dependence of the enterprise on its underpinning telecommunications and computing network is such that a responsibility sector is created in its own right to manage this area. The expenditure committed to the area makes it compatible with many other principal departments.

The emphasis in information system management is now with the user management. The IS function is responsible for data administration, facilitating the provision of information and developing the information system strategy. Although these information systems rely on data that is captured, processed, held and transmitted over the computer/telecommunication network the responsibility for data operations is conceptually quite distinct.

The organisational schema might now look like this:-

A CORPORATE COMMUNICATIONS FUNCTION

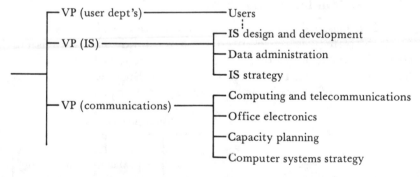

Figure 3 / 7

The manager of the computer/telecommunications function will, typically, not describe his work as computing, nor data processing, nor management information systems.

'I am in the communication business' he will say.

The VP (Communication Systems) will be responsible for the technical level hardware and related software and will have to liaise on standards and data management with the VP (Information Systems)—but their roles will be distinct.

Subsequently we will have to consider how such functions are to be planned, policies determined and strategies agreed by top management.

A New Way of Looking at Information Systems

A considerable change in management orientation must occur as an enterprise moves through the 'Seven ages of IS'. Organisational learning must occur, and restructuring of managerial authority and power becomes necessary. It is often in these organisational and personal adjustments that difficulties arise: rather more, in practice it seems, than from technical or operational problems.

It is apparent that the study of the management of information is a complex topic. What we need now, to pursue this review of effective information management, is a shared view of the field. Consequently we will use a very simple model of IS. Like all simple models it is inadequate and incomplete, but it will serve its purpose by facilitating our review.

Three Levels of Information System

The classical conception of organisation and the formulation of strategy is represented by a pyramid. This view is enshrined in most books on strategy and accepted without question by most managers. It reflects the Harvard Business School view of business policy, and was initiated by Anthony.

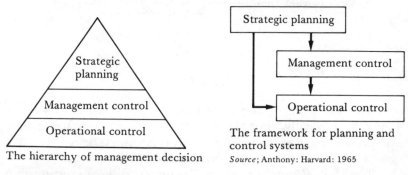

The hierarchy of management decision

The framework for planning and control systems
Source; Anthony: Harvard: 1965

Figure 3/8   *Figure 3/9*

Unfortunately in the modern complex organisation this neat, militaristic, configuration seldom fits the reality. A more convenient model might be of a barrel of resources which must be controlled on a day to day basis under the policy guide-lines of corporate strategy, which is influenced by a turbulent and ambiguous environment.

Under conditions facing modern management the strategy and the control tend to become more remote from the resources.

Managers must manage resources that are geographically spread and organisationally diverse. Between the decision maker and the resources lie systems—of people and data-handling equipment—systems that can distort, delay, amplify, dampen messages.

Figure 3/10

External to the enterprise interest groups—in government, consumers, labour representatives, international agencies and elsewhere, exercise an information exchange. The modern manager must be capable of managing his information systems.

But what is this 'information system'. Is it the computer based hardware, or the data in the files, or is it, rather, some conceptualisation of the applications in terms of the organisational needs for information? Considerable confusion has arisen from a failure to distinguish different levels of system and different types of problem.

Here we will adopt a three-layer model to help us understand the issues (fig. 3/11). Basically it is argued that information systems can usefully be considered at technical, operational and organisational levels.

The technical level

The task of the technical level system is to provide facilities for the capture, processing, transmission and communication of data for legitimate use anywhere in the organisation. Consequently it covers all telecommunications, computers and related devices (with the possible exception of equipment dedicated solely to process applications such as numerical control machines)

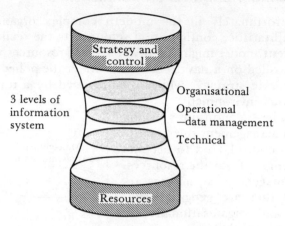

Figure 3/11

and the relevant software and support systems. In other words, the technical level covers the 'plumbing'.

- In a manufacturing company components are produced in plants around the world. The supply, manufacturing and assembly logistics are co-ordinated
  centrally, to meet customer orders from around the
  world. The company has a Head Office executive, at
  a high level in the organisation, with responsibility
  for the entire computing and communication systems
  world-wide. His approval is required before any division can lease or buy equipment for computing or
  telecommunications. A recent expenditure approval
  for corporate-wide systems was for over £20 million.
  He is concerned, primarily, with technical level
  systems.

Proper concerns at the technical level are for the creation of technical systems that are effective and efficient and which will bear the loads demanded at appropriate levels of service, reliability and cost. There are likely to be attempts at determining an optimum structure for the communication and computer systems, recognising the changing load patterns and communication costs between locations. Concern will be felt for uniformity in operating protocols and input/output devices. There is likely to be an overall plan for network operations. Dealings with computer mainframe and peripheral vendors can be co-ordinated.

The sort of problem faced is whether to use private lines or direct-dial facilities in parts of the telecommunications network; or whether one division's request for a mini-computer for a specific application is consistent with the broader corporate strategy for a larger distributed processing facility in that country. Essentially, at the technical level, we are talking about the management of computer and communications technology, both hardware and related software. Microprocessors, mini-computers and massive interrelated computing networks are all included. That does not imply that they should be under the responsibility of a single function; but that their use needs to be co-ordinated and managed.

The need for proper management planning and control at the technical level is fundamental. Increasingly computer and communications technology is becoming as fundamental to the operation and survival of any business, as aircraft are to an airline, or ovens to a bakery. Professional management of the systems at the technical level is becoming synonymous with operational and financial viability. The longer term plans at the technical level are formulated in a computer strategy.

But, it is argued, the problems and opportunities at the technical level are different in nature from those at the operational or organisational levels. We confuse them at our peril.

The operational/data management level

The task at the operational/data management level is to manage the data resource. Consequently the concerns tend to be about the capture, storage and processing of data. The content and structure of files, the rights of access to data, security and privacy of data become important.

The data management level is particularly important in data-based information systems in which both transaction-based application programmes and *ad hoc* enquiries from different parts of the business access the data-base.

Although the data management level, obviously, is dependent on the technical level for its operations, the management issues will often be quite independent. The data management level systems can be run on different configurations at the technical level—just as the content of a telephone message between London and New York is independent of the technical route via submarine cable or satellite.

It is not unusual for executives to perceive problems at the data management level as technical level problems to be met by 'upgrading the mainframe' or 'distributing the processing with front-ending minis'—whereas the reality lies in the file structure and the right to update and access the files.

There is a fundamental difference in focus between the two levels. The technical concern is with the technical facilities. At the data management level attention is directed to the user rather than to the equipment. In many cases the user will be responsible for the data and will have a sense of ownership. It will be 'my system', as we shall see in chapter 5.

The organisational level

As the name suggests the task at the organisational level is the organisation of the enterprise. The concerns here are with the definition of organisational boundaries, the identification of groupings with decision-making authority, responsibility and accountability. Management control systems, performance measures and the way the corporate goals are to be achieved are important.

- A government department considered putting the collection of cost data into the geographically remote regions. It recognised that this would enable the regional managers to control costs more directly. But it also implied a passing of authority to initiate actions previously requiring central sanction. Some officers at the centre opposed this development, arguing that it implied a loss of control. This is an example of an organisational level problem.

- An insurance company, with highly centralised technical level systems, saw the Head Office as 'the administrative factory doing the paperwork, with the regions responsible for selling'. The regional executives argued that they were not getting the information they needed to do their job efficiently. If they were given this information, which technically and operationally would be straightforward, the Head Office would have been faced with demands for wider discretion at the local level.

- A grocery chain introduced point of sale terminals at its check-out stations. It received a union demand for upgrading the job of the operators, as they were now responsible for inputs to the corporate systems.

The alternatives that are feasible at the technical level and the opportunities at the data management level provide new options at the organisational level for creating a structure and adopting a management style that the executives think are consistent with their strategies. They might shift towards greater central oversight of corporate affairs or devolve power to decide towards the periphery of their organisation. Provided, that is, that the executives recognise the opportunities and are competent in selecting appropriate alternatives.

A possible effect of changes at the technical and data management level is to destabilise the organisation. Board level executives, having been brought up in conditions in which such issues did not arise, can be organisationally incompetent, despite their enthusiasm and confidence in computing.

Another problem is likely to be the management in data-processing, once the agents of change, who find the balance of power over the corporate data swinging towards the user, and become conservative and resistant to change in consequence.

The Need for a Systems Strategy

The development of a computer based system used to be purely an operational matter. It was an area for technical experts. Top management approval and commitment were necessary if the project was to succeed; and a careful cost justification was important. But fundamentally such computer systems were not of strategic importance to the business.

Now all that has changed. The development of computer and telecommunication systems throughout organisations is found to have the most significant effects on the structure of organisation, on the style of management, and on the overall strategy of the enterprise. Indeed, so significant have some such systems become, that their failure can put the survival of the firm in jeopardy.

In the next three chapters we will look, in more detail, at the three levels of information systems. Chapter 4 discusses the technical level potential; chapter 5 introduces issues at the data management level; and chapter 6 considers the organisational level impact.

Opportunities at the technical and operational levels open up new vistas of organisational alternatives. No longer need organisation structure be adapted to meet crises; it can be planned. No longer need management style emerge; it can be created. No longer should information systems be thought of as operational support mechanisms; they are of strategic significance.

But the choices should reflect the needs of the business, not the desirability of technology. An information system strategy is as important as a marketing or a financial strategy. It enables senior management to formulate their policies and plans on communication and control, organisation structure and preferred management style in their enterprise in the context of their overall formulation of strategy. It facilitates the development of computer and telecommunication systems, the professional management of the data resource and the development of managers and organisation.

Reference

1. G. F. Gibson and Richard L. Nolan: Managing the four stages of EDP growth: Harvard Business Review; January/February 1974.

4
A Technological Perspective
*•what is feasible and the need for a
computer system strategy*

'All this talk about distributed processing, satellite communication and the electronic office baffles me. We don't know
how to use the technology we've got at the moment.'

A CEO in New York

'My DP manager keeps pressing me to upgrade the computer mainframe to keep up with demands and improve the
service to the company. One of my Divisional Managers wants
approval for his own mini-computers. The DP staff are opposed.
How should I proceed?'

Managing Director of a British company

In this chapter we review the
technical level of the information
systems triplet.

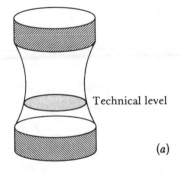

Technical level

(a)

The Economic Imperative

In many organisations the
technological potential of computers and telecommunication is
already far ahead of manage-
ment's ability to understand the implications and imagine the
alternatives. Developments that will become available in the
next few years will compound the problem.

But excitement for new technology must be set against
organisational reality. The emphasis today on funds flow and
'bottom-line' profit returns in the private sector, and cash constraints in the public, tend to temper technological enthusiasm

for its own sake. What is needed is the contribution from technology that is cost-effective in the short and the long term. The issues are predominantly managerial rather than technical.

In this chapter we will follow the evolution of computers and communication systems up to the present and indicate the potential in networked systems and office automation at the technical level—that is at the level of the 'plumbing'—the hardware and supporting software on which we drive our information systems.

As organisations grow, in size and complexity, the proportion of revenue spend on internal communication, co-ordination and control multiplies. It can be a salutory exercise in a company to calculate the total cost of computers, data-processing, telephone and telex, paper for reports and executive time in meetings and travel etc.—the total cost of communication—and observe how the percentage of total cost is increasing.

In the small, entrepreneurial enterprise, dominated by one man, communication cost is typically miniscule. Such business-

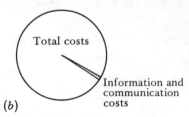

(b)

men are their own information systems. They know what is going on from personal observation. They communicate by personal contact. They co-ordinate and control their organisations; they determine and decide.

But even the simple organisation, which has functional departments and manual systems, begins to incur significant costs on internal communication.

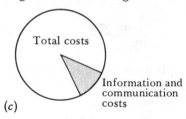

(c)

Reports have to be produced, meetings convened with minutes and agendas, and massive files and records begin to accumulate. The proportion of revenues committed to communication, co-ordination and control begins to become significant.

Now consider the complex structures and systems of many modern organisations—multi-layered, multi-faceted and multi-national. The annual spend on internal communication is large and often increasing annually. Computer and telecommunication budgets can consume anything up to 5% of total revenues. The total spend on information and information related activities is huge and highly significant— particularly in service related enterprises.

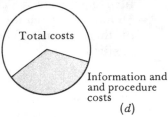

Total costs

Information and and procedure costs

(d)

Moreover, as office and executive labour rates, software development costs, telephone, postage and paper costs continue to rise, there is an economic imperative to achieve productivity improvements from expenditures on communication. Effective use of technical level opportunities can offset rising costs by more efficient operations and reducing costs of new electronic technology. But such developments need managing.

- 'The price of the office's raw material—paper—rose 87% between 1973 and 1979. It has risen by a further 26% since. The cost of producing a business letter is now reckoned to be somewhere between $5 and $8. The Yankee Group estimates there are on average about eight file drawers of information containing some 18,000 documents for every white-collar worker in America. Between them, the country's white-collar workers produce 72 billion documents annually and maintain and file another 300 billion or so. The information explosion, it seems, is proceeding at a rate of about two file drawers per office worker each year.

  Nor have communication costs escaped inflation. Even efficient (by world standards) Bell Telephone has been forced to raise telephone rates—by 160% between 1970 and 1977. Office workers in the United States currently make around 100 billion telephone calls a year, at an average cost of 15 cents per call. That adds up to $15 billion a year.

  The average manager spends 80% of his or her time just in communication—transmitting or receiving information. Another survey found that the average office professional (i.e. marketing man, accountant, statistician, lawyer etc.) wasted 20–30% of his or her

time just looking for information. The cost of a misfiled document is believed to amount to more than
$60. Firms generally misfile between 1% and 5% of
of their records. They lose permanently half those
misfiled.'

Source: The Economist

The longer term potential is to achieve savings through
effective information systems and communication automation
of the order of those achieved in the past when traditional craft
jobs in industry were automated. Similarly there is the potential
for labour dissatisfaction and job loss.

The commercial imperative at the enterprise level to achieve
improved productivity from information-related expenditure
has an interesting reflection at the macro-economic level.

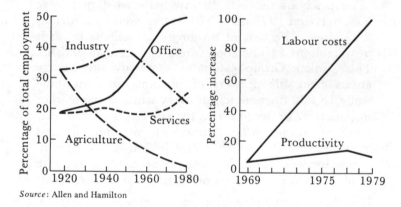

Source: Allen and Hamilton

Figure 4/1

Towards the end of the 19th century the majority of
workers were on the land. There were many in private service,
an increasing number in manufacturing but few in information
related work such as librarians or clerks. Over the century as the
diagram shows, the numbers working in the fields have fallen
dramatically. Those engaged in physical manufacture of goods,
after a significant rise, are also now falling. Those in service
functions having fallen as private service declined are now firmly
rising as government services and service industries increase.

But the dramatic change has been in those engaged in information and office related work of all types. Many jobs in the advanced world can now be classified as information activities. This is the basis for the claim of those who argue that the shift from agrarian to urban and industrial life is now being followed by a further shift to a post-industrial information society.

Japan and France, recognising the significance of information technology, have national plans for development in the field.

From Data Processing to Information Facilitating

Computer specialists tend to describe the development of computing as a succession of generations. For our purposes it will be more useful to consider the evolution of applications and their impact on the enterprise. We will chart seven successive stages, though of course their boundaries are arbitrary and any company can be at different stages in various parts. The stages are:-

1. *Manual records*
2. *Early computerisation*
3. *The attempt at integration*
4. *Information systems monitoring key resources*
5. *Data-base ideas*
6. *Networks and minis*
7. *Office automation*

1. *Manual records.* Before any computer applications, the functionally independent departments tend to keep their own records. Consequently there is duplication of effort in paper handling and recording, and there are disparities between records because of lags in entry and errors. Data from such files tends to be abstracted and reported upwards through the departmental hierarchy. Only the accountants' records run across organisational boundaries, monitoring each department, but predominantly in financial terms.

2. *Early computerisation.* Typically early application of computers involves the computerisation of the existing manual records, within existing organisational boundaries. Payroll,

billing/invoicing, ledger accounting, inventory records are typical examples of such batch orientated systems. The justification for these projects will usually be in terms of direct cost savings, perhaps in clerical labour or in the cost of alternative bureau processing.

Interestingly, with the advent of very cheap, yet powerful, small computers there has been a resurgence of companies at this level, mainly small themselves, coming to computer assistance for the first time. Moreover many of them seem to be making the classical errors which the large computer users were making ten or twenty years ago—almost always in terms of management failure to be involved, to plan, control and manage effectively.

3.   *The attempt at integration.*   As computer applications multiply in a firm there is a tendency for them to cross the existing organisational boundaries. The output from one system becomes the input data for another. For example, the data from order-entry files is needed to update the production or dispatch systems, which generate data for invoicing, inventory control and management costing systems.

Justification for computer projects, at this stage, is frequently in terms of improved performance—improved customer service, for example, or lower inventories with fewer 'stock-outs'.

Observing the trend towards integrated systems, some writers in the 1960s began to predict the ultimate 'total information system'. Once all the data flows and all the files had been computerised, they argued, there would be an overall integration or total information system. Such prognostications failed to appreciate the real distinction between data and information, and are generally recognised today as naive. Those companies that tried to build such totally integrated systems soon found that they were designing the nervous system for an industrial dinosaur.

The author was involved in one such endeavour in the 1960s. An enormous flow chart, in excrutiating detail, was drawn of the existing data flows and use. The job of developing the computer-based system then began. It soon became apparent that all was not well, when the system chief designer asked for a memo to be sent to all departmental heads—'There are to be no changes to your organisation and no new demands for information for the next two years, until our system is built'.

4. *Information systems monitoring key resources.* The really significant achievements in computer-based systems came when the applications began to monitor and support the key resources and fundamental processes of the organisation—seat reservation systems in airlines, patient records in hospitals, inventory and distribution in market-orientated firms, logistics of manufacturing companies, or customer-accounting in banks. The computer-based information system was becoming a key element in the operations of the enterprise.

Justification for the system was now in terms of improved efficiency in the enterprise. In many cases it was now no longer possible to revert to a manual system: if the computer system stopped, so did the business operations.

Over the years, of course, the technology had developed to facilitate such applications. Instead of a technical level system of peripherals and storage devices grouped around a central processing unit (CPU) in a glass partitioned enclosure (as in stage 2 or 3), the technical systems now involved large computer systems, with remote terminals and more than one CPU.

5. *Data-base ideas.* The further technical level development that permitted access to common files of data by different application programmes or for ad hoc enquiries added a new dimension—the data base concept.

Essentially data is captured at source, subjected to controls for relevance, validation and accuracy, and input to the data-base once only. No longer does each application programme have to have its separate input and maintain its independent set of files.

Under the data-base idea the data is stored in a structured set of common files, where it can be addressed, element by element, for use in application programmes and for ad hoc enquiries. Moreover the structure of the data-base is independent of the application use.

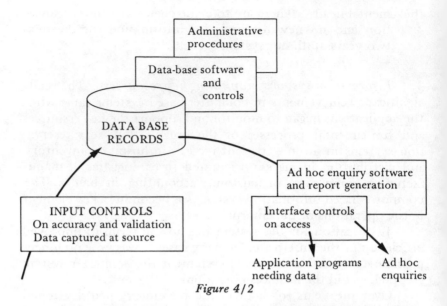

Figure 4/2

For example, the personnel records of one of the armed forces are held on a data-base. Considerable data about each member—name, number, personal details, availability, location, pay data, training information, postings to date and so on—are kept in the file.

Each man's record is, in effect, a sequential string of data, with the various elements individually addressable.

Thus the payroll application can call up just his name, number, pay data and location when producing the salary list.

Alternatively a user can address the data-base for an answer to questions such as—'locate those men, under 30, currently in the UK and available for overseas postings, who speak Arabic and have at least 100 hours training and experience of engine maintenance'.

In the data-base situation the security of the data-base and the integrity of the data become important issues. Tight controls and procedures are necessary on input, to ensure that only those with approved authority amend, add to or delete records. Professional procedures are vital to oversee the administration of the data-base, including the responsibility for physical security and the ability to recreate files if losses occur. Then, obviously, controls are necessary on the right of access to the data and on priority of access. In the next chapter we will look at the management of the data resource.

6. *Networks and minis.*   The range of options at the technical level in computing and the communication systems is now legion. No longer need the configuration be CPU centred, and telecommunication and computing have tended to merge at one end of the scale; and opportunities have become vast in stand-alone mini-computers and micro-processors at the other end.

Now a new set of managerial problems arises. What configuration of equipment, at the technical level, is most suitable for the needs of the organisation. Let us look briefly, and conceptually, at the range of options.

At one end of the scale is the *Centralised System.* Data-processing and data storage are centralised, perhaps with other computers providing communication and message switching capabilities, to link terminal devices throughout the organisation—which may be global in scale. The terminals have only limited processing and storage capacity, if any, on their own. They will not function independently of the main network.

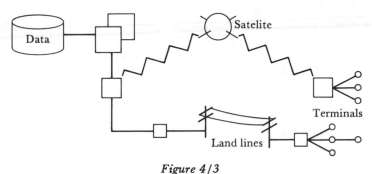

Figure 4/3

Typically such systems are dedicated to specific tasks, for example, airlines seat reservations, bank accounting or police records.

Then one can consider the technical level system with *the intelligent terminal.* Now the local station has a terminal facility with relatively limited data-processing and storage capabilities, linked to the main capacity and data storage. Here there is greater flexibility to process jobs and hold records locally. But the facility to link-up, either continuously or periodically, to the central records and large scale processing facilitates overall control and co-ordinated records.

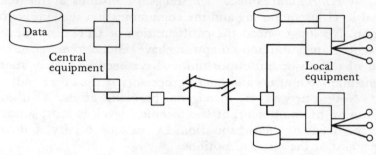

Figure 4/4

A more complex development, giving greater local autonomy, whilst maintaining central options is found in *distributed processing*. Here there are host and satellite computers in a network. Local responsibility for data collection and processing, and the keeping of local files can be balanced against centralised processing and record keeping.

Such technical level configurations are likely to be multipurpose, and not dedicated to specific tasks. The choice of configuration, is, obviously, a highly complex and specialised task. However, broadly, the arguments for a distributed processing

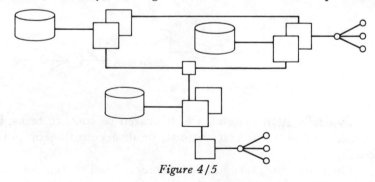

Figure 4/5

system against a more centralised system run as follows:-

For a distributed processing system:	*Against:*
• Data-processing is located where it can be carried out most efficiently and most cheaply.	The use of the local processors is less efficient and it is not necessarily cheaper.
• Transmission costs of a centralised system are saved.	Transmission costs are not necessarily less.
• Cost control can be exercised in local modules. Costs are more visible.	More intricate networks increase costs. Costs cannot be controlled centrally.
• The system is less vulnerable and thus more reliable.	CPU usage is reduced. It is less efficient.
• Local interest is encouraged. Problems can be solved locally.	Suboptimisation occurs. Local stations duplicate staff, programmes and overheads.
• Data accuracy is improved through local responsibility.	Data cannot be administered effectively.
• The costs of central controls can be reduced. Less bureaucracy.	The central control on standards, codes, processes and procedures, often painfully developed throughout organisations, can be eroded and lost.
• Provides co-ordination without domination. 'Small is beautiful.'	Removes the opportunity of central control. 'Overall control is optimal.'

• As an example of a distributed data processing network consider the Philips system that is supplied to the Dutch government, and that is spread throughout that country.

The system installed for the Ministry of Finance at present comprises more than 130 PTS 6805 terminal computers which form the connection with the communication network. Linked to these are some 260 work-stations, each consisting of a visual display unit, keyboard and printer. The communication network itself is built up from six mini-computers, five acting as line concentrators and one as the network processor. Planned expansion in the early 1980s will increase the number of work-stations to 750.

Finally, at the end of the range furthest from the centralised systems are *stand-alone mini-computers.* Here the management

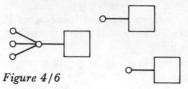

Figure 4/6

have chosen a computer strategy which enables each potential user to acquire, or have access to, his own independent equipment. The reducing hardware costs of such computers makes this a feasible proposition; although increasing software development costs have also to be considered. Obviously, in such a situation, direct communication between the equipment or with a central computer is not possible. Communication is through the messenger or the mail service.

Today many small computers have processing power equivalent to the mainframe CPUs of the earlier generations, have sophisticated storage and are, by comparison, very cheap. The software packages to undertake many applications are also becoming available and reliable.

The strategy for computers and telecommunications at the technical level has now become an important managerial task. As we shall see as we explore the higher levels of information system, choices made at the technical level can inhibit or facilitate opportunities in data-management and organisation structure and style.

7.   *Office automation.*   Finally, in this brief over-view of the evolution of computer and communication system applications at the technical level we turn to the frontier topic, for even the more advanced and experienced users of computers. Office electronics or the 'Office of the Future' has figured in many promotions and promises from equipment manufacturers. But it is an area for speculation and experimentation rather than wide-spread experience. Developments are at an early stage, although the next few years will undoubtedly see major advances. Let us review briefly some of the component features of office automation.

Word processing uses either dedicated word processors or small computers with word processing software to facilitate the typing of letters and reports with common elements, to produce personalised mailings and facilitate the work of the typing pool. *Text editing* is an application of word processing, in which the author, the editor and the typist can adapt and revise a text, such as a report or a book, using the video screen rather than repetitively typing onto paper. It also obviates the need for repetitive proof-reading. A communication facility can be added so that material prepared in one location can be typed out at another. By linking offices, internationally where appropriate, a form of *electronic mail* is provided.

Voice mail is another technical level system that some experts believe will have a big impact. Basically this involves a computer data-base hooked into the telephone system which will store voice messages and deliver them at a predetermined future time or when a recipient is available. Such a system would eliminate time wasted in futile telephone calls. Interestingly the equipment converts the voice data to digital data for storage, when it can be handled just like word processing data and further developments can be expected. Obviously such a system will not replace urgent calls that need a dialogue: but will substitute for much time-wasting routine calls.

Reprographics is a term used to cover the automation of the printing and duplicating function. For example, word processors can be linked to *photo-composition equipment* which produces plates for printing machinery. Also the *communicating copier* can be linked to data or word processing equipment to print output from these computers at high speed and with a variety of formats.

Equipment, with associated software, for generating *graphics*, both on screen and paper, and often in colour, offers the potential for improving communication of complex data and difficult ideas. A graphics work station can be programmed to produce line and bar graphs, pie diagrams, logarithmic charts and overhead projector transparencies.

Linking office stations by a communication network can provide visual communication of text and figures, in the same way that a telephone network provides for audio communication. This not only facilitates *facsimile transmission* of reports and the provision of an electronic mail service, but opens the way for *computer conferencing*.

The participants in a computer conference are connected to a data-base and a network of people sharing common interests in the subject of the conference. Participants share in a dialogue via the data-base, with each other. Items of common interest are pooled, and questions and answers exchanged. Each participant connects at any time suitable to him, irrespective of the other users, in effect producing a perpetual dialogue. Computer conferences are proving useful to scientists, development engineers and project managers—groups who share a common interest and need to be kept in touch with what is happening and with each other. They provide a continuing, stored and retrievable dialogue.

If the quality of the communication channels is sufficiently high, signals of TV quality can be transmitted, enabling the exchange of pictures in *video transmission*. Such video pictures can, of course, also be stored on video tape and disk.

Another development in the video exchange is the *teleconference* or *videoconference*. Instead of travelling to meetings, participants are joined together from their own offices or specially designed, local stations. They see each other on TV monitors either in full motion like a normal TV picture or in a, less expensive, frame by frame exposure changing every ten seconds or so.

> Some hotel chains, such as Holiday Inns in the US, have installed dish antennae at various hotels to catch satellite TV and 'Home Box Office' movies for guests. This equipment, it has been suggested, could also form the basis for a teleconferencing service.

Developments in storage media, called *micrographics*, also offer some important opportunities. Instead of printing computer output onto paper, which is increasing in cost, the output is recorded directly onto a microform (*computer onto microform or COM*). Aperture cards, microfiche and film jackets have replaced the conventional microfilm roll, which can be easily read on a simple reader and readily carried.

Computer-aided retrieval (CAR) combines the benefits of micrographics and computers for storage and retrieval purposes. Instead of manually filing papers, CAR equipment stores the images on microform very cheaply and uses the computer to search and retrieve the record. Indexes kept by computer can be quite elaborate, facilitating logical searches of some complexity. The automation of records management is the longer term aim.

- Exxon has combined the use of microfilm storage and magnetic storage in several key company locations to streamline the handling of incoming correspondence.

  Before reaching the addressee, an incoming letter is indexed, abstracted and the abstracted information entered into magnetic storage. The letter is then recorded on updated microfiche, and forwarded, along with the fiche, to the addressee.

  Every subsequent piece of incoming, outgoing or internal communication related to that document is added in abstract form to magnetic storage, and as a complete image on the updatable microfiche. Thus, each incoming letter goes to the addressee accompanied by a fiche of all the correspondence to date pertaining to the subject of the letter.

  At any time, then, an Exxon executive can call for the complete file on a given project by calling up the abstracted information from magnetic storage or the complete pages from microfiche, and viewing the file on a screen. Further, microfiche copies of correspondence abstracts on any subject are distributed to every executive on a regular basis.

The opportunity to access data-bases using a local video screen, over communication lines, has important implications. For example, car dealers can discover the location of a specific model that a customer wants, retail companies can make credit enquiries, travel agents can retrieve information on airlines, hotels, hire cars and make reservations, and ultimately individuals will be able to conduct their banking, mail-order and many other transactions via their home terminal. We will explore these issues in the next chapter, when we consider the data management level of information systems.

The potential for linking office automation with process automation in manufacturing plants has also to be recognised.

Trends in office automation. A study of developments in leading companies, on both sides of the Atlantic, suggests that developments are currently piecemeal. Significant cost advantages may be attainable from office automation as unit costs are reduced; although currently savings in hardware and software expenditure may not be so readily attained. As the VP (Information Systems) for a large US company remarked 'this is still a green field site for development'.

There may be important constraints in achieving anticipated savings from office automation. Firstly, there are people issues—resistance to change from managers, unions, works councils and individuals involved. Reductions in staff are feasible but freeing people for more productive roles may be more desirable. Secondly, there may be a lack of understanding of the precise way in which the organisation works making the application of information technology ineffective.

Some companies have a building block plan to develop their automated office piece by piece. They recognise that, at the technical level, new developments are imminent. Consequently they justify their projects on a three to five year horizon, recognising that such costs may have to be written off. They also know that the important issues will involve rethinking the way the firm organises itself and manages its information.

'Don't fall into the same trap as early computing applications of automating the existing jobs—rethink the organisation.'
Wise words from a DP executive

Some significant trends in office automation can be anticipated:

Firstly *CONVERGENCE OF EQUIPMENT*, as electronic chip technology and agreement on communication protocols facilitate interaction between pieces of equipment. The emphasis is likely to be on user-friendly terminals which shift the opportunities for creating 'his own' system towards the user. The office ringmain concept would then begin to unite the various systems.

The next stage would then be seen as a *UNIFICATION OF EQUIPMENT*. Instead of having two, three or more terminals to access different systems, which is the trend today, the user would have a single terminal (perhaps a keyboard, screen and hard-copy printer) to access many systems.

INTEGRATION OF USE would be achieved when the personal computer terminal, or *executive work station* as it is sometimes called, became a practical possibility.

A lot of work is being done in this area. Ultimately the user would be able to receive and send messages via his screen

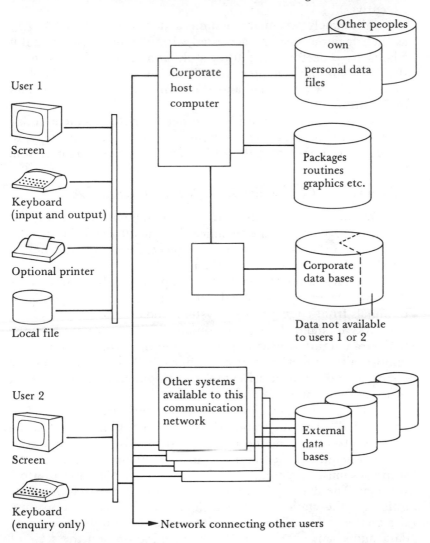

Figure 4/7

(electronic mail), access his own private files and give access to them to others, access those parts of the corporate files that are open to him, access any external data-bases subscribed to by the company, call on graphical display, statistical routines and modelling facilities to manipulate the data, and report to other executives.

Ultimately we might assume a degree of *ASSIMILATION* as such facilities become accepted within an organisation and it adapts its processes, structure, style and expectations to meet them. In the final chapter we will review some of the implications of the 'wired-office' and the 'wired-city' for management in the future.

We should now consider the need for management today to develop a computer and communication systems strategy, to manage developments at the technical level in their organisation.

Computer and Communication Systems Strategy

We have seen in this chapter that there are many options facing management at the technical level in information systems. There is no shortage of alternative pieces of equipment nor of manufacturers anxious to sell them.

We have noted the range of computer configurations now available, from large centralised systems, through intelligent terminals front-ending central systems and distributed processing networks to stand-alone mini-computers. We have seen how the basic transaction processing application has evolved to become opportunities for information facilitating. We have also seen the increasing opportunities for buying equipment and software for office automation projects.

Obviously such investments at the technical level need to be planned, controlled and managed. 'The plumbing' must be adequate too and consistent with the demands placed upon it.

Consequently computer and communication systems strategies must be a component in the overall information system strategy. The data operations and the organisational levels must influence the choices at the technical level; just as opportunities at the technical level can give new opportunities to manage data and change the structure of organisation and the style of management.

5
A Data-operations Perspective
●*managing managements' crucial resource*

'Simple questions do not beget simple answers.'

Dewey

'He who knows the price of every thing and the value of nothing is a cynic.'

Oscar Wilde

'Everything should be made as simple as possible; but not simpler.'

Albert Einstein

In this chapter we consider the management of the data resource —the second level in the information system structure.

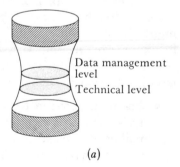

Information, as we saw earlier, involves a process in which data is used. It is a function of data, the user and the user's situation. This applies to all levels of decision from the most short-term, operational choices to very long-term strategic decisions.

(a)

- The pilot flying Concorde must make rapid decisions. He needs immediate data. Indeed some fighter planes travel so fast that the pilot has data displayed on the windscreen so that he need not glance down at the instruments.

75

Operating level decisions, involved in flying a plane, driving a car and many routine day to day activities, have relatively short time horizons, little ambiguity and draw their data from a limited set of sources. Sometimes such decisions can be programmed, the rules worked out, for computerisation.

- An automatic landing system, in which an on-board computer receives data from the landing beam, to bring the plane safely onto the runway in thick fog, is an example of a machine using data to become informed and take decisions.

At higher levels of decision, time horizons are longer, ambiguity greater and more sources of data need to be scanned.

- In deciding what action to take when facing a possible major fluctuation in a raw material price, basic to his business, a manager has many factors to take into account—the effect on cash flow, the possible shortage of supply, alternative materials, competitor actions, warehouse requirements, labour implications, and so on.

In making management decisions the executive needs data from within his business, but also from the external environment. As decisions become strategic in significance, their time horizons can become very long, considerable uncertainty and risk is involved and the source of the basic data is likely to be largely external to the enterprise.

- Facing a decision to launch a new consumer product, let's say a frozen croissant, the strategic decision makers will have to consider what factors they think are important in reaching their decisions, and what things might affect the outcome, before they can begin to determine their information needs.

As we consider the relevance of data in an enterprise we shall need to keep this scale of decisions in our mind. The data must be apposite to the decision makers' needs. But one thing is clear: in modern organisations, typified by change, ambiguity, turbulence and scale, data has become a vital resource. No longer able to make personal contact with all the factors involved, the decision maker needs to receive data through communication channels as the basis of being informed.

In the past the cost of data handling and processing was an overhead to be controlled, and reduced where possible: now data has become a resource to be managed professionally. What was an expense has become an asset.

Sources of Data

Data can usefully be categorised by its source—whether it is internal or external to the enterprise; and whether it is provided by formal, routine systems or by ad-hoc and non-routine means.

Formal	A	C
Informal	B	D
	Internal	External

Source of data

Figure 5/1

Although the entrepreneur operates primarily in quadrant D, the bulk of corporate information systems lie in quadrant A; that is they are formal, transaction orientated systems monitoring internal factors. The potential of information systems, however, is to facilitate the information process in each quadrant. Let us consider how.

A. *Data—internal and formal.* All enterprises have certain key resources that must be measured and monitored so that their state and changes are known. Consequently the principal formal records tend to reflect such resources. In an airline they are the seat reservation files, in a steel works the files of orders and production logistics, in a hospital the patient records, in a bank the customer accounts, in a wholesaling business the inventory records and so on.

Such files are an integral part of the operations of the enterprise. Great care is likely to be given to their accuracy, currency and security. Without them the business cannot operate. Rules will be laid down to determine who has the responsibility to update and amend such records and who has a right of access. Auditors will be concerned about the ability to check transactions through such records.

In addition to the key files, a network of related, transaction-based records will also be created, in the typical enterprise, to support the basic operations.

To date the dominant contribution of computer-based information systems has been in quadrant A.

B. *Data—internal and informal.* It is obvious, however, that the bulk of data communicated in an organisation is not formal but moves by personal contact and telephone. Predominantly it is not even seen, let alone written down and computerised.

Yet the potential for computer and telecommunication support to the internal and informal data processes is considerable. The development of user-friendly retrieval languages is facilitating the ad-hoc enquiry of those internal corporate files that are to be available to a given user. Some command languages now being developed are easy to use, being on-line with a minimum of key-strokes at a terminal and responsive to the non-expert user by tolerating errors and helping the user search for the data he needs.

In such circumstances the integrity of the data-bases can be centrally controlled, though accessibility is widespread. We will discuss the management of the data-base and the use of information centres to facilitate the search of corporate data later.

What is occurring in advanced computer-based systems is a continuation of the structured and application orientated systems in quadrant A but with a gradual segmentation and the provision of on-line command languages to meet the data needs of the distributed user in quadrant B.

The extension of the executive work station, described in the last chapter will, of course, facilitate the developments in this sector.

C. *Data—external and formal.* Some organisations have made significant investments in developing data-bases internally that monitor details of activities and resources external to the business. For example, a merchant banking company has a major data-base of company profiles that it can monitor when seeking possible acquisition opportunities for a client; automobile manufacturers frequently keep files of cars held by their distributors and agents, enabling the ready provision of a vehicle to a customer's precise requirements; some travel agents have developed records of vacation and conference facilities to respond to client questions, some also keep profiles of their main clients' travel requirements.

The technology is available to support such data bases. The crucial factor is obtaining access to reliable, current and accurate data about the relevant external feature. But the great area of growth, and the one with enormous potential, is access to data-bases that are held externally to the enterprise by organisations that offer access facilities.

D.   *Data—external and informal.*   Opportunities for accessing external data on an ad-hoc, as needed, basis are soaring. The selling of data, or the right of access to data, is becoming an important industry.

We need a means of typifying the various services on offer. Consider them in terms of the ability to enquire and whether the user can update the files.

		Teledata	Datanet
	No	Teledata	Datanet
Enquiry facility	Yes	Videotext	Conferencing and information utility
		No	Yes
		Updating facility	

The Information Supermarket

Figure 5/2

TELEDATA.   In these types of service the user has access to whatever is on offer, but the communication process is one way only. A good example is the CEEFAX service of the BBC which enables anyone with the appropriate TV receiver to pick up the data being transmitted continuously. The ITV equivalent is called ORACLE. The user may select from a 'menu' of data on subjects such as the latest news, stock market prices, weather, theatre, etc. But the selection is by isolating the data being transmitted; it does not permit a search of the files because the communication channel is one way only.

Teledata type of services over land lines include the many newspaper wire services that are available, and news services such as horse racing prices and results for betting shops in Britain. Stock market, commodity, currency and gold prices are also available to subscribers over land lines.

DATANET. These services are similar to the Teledata type of facility—in only providing access to specific data files and not permitting searches of those files. However, the user may update the files from his remote location. Some theatre and airline/shipping/rail seat reservation systems operate this way, with the local agent able to access the file to discover availability and to make specific reservations. Stock availability systems in use in some industries, such as automobile distribution, are also examples of the DATANET type.

VIDEOTEXT. In these services the user has two-way communication with the provider of the service and may search the files but may not update them.

> Consider the PRESTEL system available in Britain. Essentially the equipment is a PRESTEL TV set that is connected to the user's telephone line. The range of data is immense. Over 200,000 pages are currently available, which are updated and enlarged continuously by over 300 independent providers of information. For example, British Airways lists its flight departures and seat prices. Amongst the vast amount of data are files on world news, management consultants, exchange rates, company results, sport, hotels, real estate available, consumer goods, parliament, stock exchange prices, employment by region, entertainment, economic indicators, European farm news, restaurants, architects design criteria, and local news by region. PTTs in West Germany, Holland and Switzerland have bought the British Telecom software and knowhow.

PRESTEL is easy to instal and can be attached to any TV set and any telephone socket. An extension of the concept enables a user to become a 'closed user group' tranforming individual sets into an internal visual communication system for monitoring sales and stocks, sending internal memos and communicating throughout a network of users; and upgrading the facility to an information utility.

In Canada the INFOGLOBE system has over 250,000 articles in its data-base from staff writers of the Globe and Mail newspaper. It can be accessed by telephone or directly via the TELENET and TYMNET data networks in North America or by telephone packet switching internationally.

The French are working on a telephone directory project, providing telephone subscribers with a screen and keyboard. Such a network would facilitate Videotext services.

In the USA the TELIDON system has many of the essential features of PRESTEL with specialised terminals to facilitate its incorporation into systems of office automation.

In order to promote the exchange of scientific, technical, and socio-economic information between the member states of the European Community, the European Commission has initiated the Euronet DIANE network. Euronet is a Europe wide data transmission network built by the Post and Telecommunication authorities (the PTTs) to give on-line access to the DIANE (Direct Information Access Network for Europe) set of data-bases.

The user's equipment for DIANE consists of a terminal fitted with a visual display and printer connected to the telephone network via a modem. Interestingly, communication costs are not based on distance but on connection time and the volume of data transmitted. Thus, where the 'host' data-base may be held is immaterial.

Using Euronet DIANE:

Users are provided with a directory which lists each of the host data-bases, from ARDIC (a chemistry and spectroscopy base in Paris) through the British library information service in London, CERVED (commercial data in Rome), the European Patents Office, the European Space Agency,

GID (R & D data in Frankfurt) and many more to THERMO-DATA (thermodynamic data in France).

The user connects to the network by dialing an access number. The host is then called up by keying in his address and the user's identification number.

A password is used for security and accounting purposes. Then the user conducts a dialogue with the host data-base, searching for the information required.

For example, the user wants to discover what is on record about alcohol as a replacement fuel. He keys in 'fuel' and 'replacement'. The host indicates 785 items containing these key words. The user adds the word 'alcohol' and the number of references is reduced to 38. These 38 items are then called up, either on the screen or the printer, in detail—or the user can ask for them to be sent by post if they are lengthy.

Such systems facilitate information searches. In due course the number of data-bases that may be accessed will be legion. The implications for business, and for society, have still to be understood.

CONFERENCING AND THE INFORMATION UTILITY.

Finally we come to the facility which permits two-way access to a multitude of files and the opportunity to update and supplement such records.

There are two types of computer/tele-conferencing. In the first, various sets of users, usually separated by considerable distances (otherwise they would meet in person) are connected by sophisticated, high quality television circuits that permit audio-visual interaction and the exchange of facsimile documents. We will consider some possible social and economic implications in chapter 10.

The second type of computer conferencing involves the creation of a 'club' of users interested in a specific topic. It might be brain surgery, econometrics or chess, but through the network the members exchange details of their own work, can ask questions of other members and generally, can keep in touch with the subject through the club—without ever meeting or otherwise corresponding with other members.

Some computer conferences are 'public'; that is they are open to anyone interested in the subject. The members will probably be unknown to one another. Others are private, being an 'in' group of enthusiasts.

The potential in this sector has much still to be realised. Since two-way communication is possible and users may create or add to files, in effect the other three quadrants of the matrix are incorporated. Now a user may search for data himself; may ask 'is anyone working on . . .', or 'does anyone know the source of . . .'; may exchange information and ideas through effective communication channels; may even become involved in a dialogue with various other users—a sort of computer-assisted brainstorming. The outcome of such 'many-to-many' communications have yet to be clearly appreciated.

Decision Support Systems

A concept which has raised considerable interest, particularly among American academics, is the decision support system. The underlying idea is that, unlike transaction processing systems, the decision support system will provide a model of some process or situation, as well as data about it, so that the user can explore the consequences of different actions.

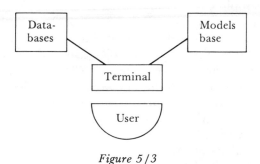

Figure 5/3

Obviously the data-base must be accessible by an appropriate data-base enquiry system. Then the user might be able to call on statistical routines and mathematical models to explore relationships in the data. Accounting models might be provided to test, for example, the cash flow implications of certain assumptions; or they might be process or other organisational models that he can use. Then graphical and other report formatting methods may be available to him.

Many software packages now offer statistical routines and various types of similation modelling. Financial simulation is widespread, varying from the simplest model of cash budgeting to complex, interactive models of corporate performance.

Essentially the user is able to call up past data and ask: 'what if such and such circumstances occurred?' when looking to the future.

- A Los Angeles based manufacturer of plastic pipe fittings increased its inventory turn from less than 3 to 3.7 and raised its on-time deliveries from 10% to 94%; also adding $500,000 to operating profit by determining the most profitable product mix for nearly 4,000 different fittings from operational planning models.

- National Airlines, in the USA, is saving millions of dollars annually, by using a fuel management and flight allocation model.

- 'National also kept its flights on schedule during the recent fuel shortages, while compensating for fluctuating supplies and rising costs, thanks to the speed at which its computer model can mirror changing business conditions. The airline stores data on fuel prices and availability, along with storage costs and fuel capacity at each of the 30 cities it serves. The performance and tentative monthly itinerary are also included for each of its 56 aircraft. In just 15 minutes the computer produces a list of the best fueling stations and vendors for each flight, something that used to take a month to do manually. 'We used to make up a schedule once a month', the Manager of Systems and Data Services says, 'but now we can run it two or three times a week.'

Source: Business Week

The concept of the decision support system, for some, is a useful, generic phrase to describe the facilities that are already being used; for others it is a concept still to be realised in practice, involving complex modeling and mathematical processes; for yet others it is another name for the executive work station idea that we have already discussed.

The White House Experience

Shortly after President Carter was elected to the Presidency of the United States he set up a team to study ways of improving the information processes in the Oval Office—the heart of Presidential decision making. Their conclusions, published after his Presidency had come to an end, make interesting reading (1).

> 'In spite of the obvious and conventional improvements, progress toward the important goals of freeing Presidential decision making from establishment dependency and improving decision making has not been affected directly by information systems. This is not surprising. The same results have failed to materialise in the senior management activities of other large organisations, industrial or governmental.

> Let us examine in more detail what Richard Harden, the President's Special Assistant for Information Management, has tried to do. One concept advanced by Harden soon after taking over O.A. was that a system of terminals would improve the flow of information within the E. O. P. and provide easier access to files and computers.

> While it is true that a network of terminals (with appropriate protocol translation) could make data files and computers more accessible to users, it is questionable whether or not this network, in turn, would make *information* for policy analysis or decision making more accessible. Most of the data for policy analysis are gathered from many diverse sources (few of which, in practice, are machine readable) and the information content is the interpretation made by the participants in the policy formulation process. In a sense, information is part of the process; it is an interaction among the participants, rather than an entity itself.

Furthermore, there is an assumption that has not been substantiated. The assumption that *more* information (or even better information, if that could be defined) leads to better decisions is open to question . . .

'Policy analysis is a specific, demanding activity requiring many years of training. By the time a policy analyst (in either the public or private sector) reaches a top post, he or she has developed data sources, contacts, analytic and interpretative skills. The key elements are the richness of the set of action alternatives considered and the accuracy with which the consequences of action alternatives are forecast. These skills cannot easily be replaced or augmented by a computer system.'

'. . . the other possible use of a network in the E.O.P.: to provide an electronic mail or message service. As far as discussions on critical policy issues are concerned, most communications, particularly on intermediate levels, take place orally in pairs or in groups. Under these conditions it is questionable if linking White House staff members together with a computer based message system would improve their ability to communicate with each other, or if they want a record of such discussions.'

'There are usually some executive activities within any organisation that do lend themselves to the development of a computer based decision support system. Such activities are characterised by *repetitive decisions* where the *values* for the parameters on which the decision will be based can be determined in advance, and the parameters can be related to an *analytic* manner. One example of such a system within the E.O.P. is the interactive analysis system developed by S.T.R. to assist trade negotiators: others are the budget systems.'

The War Room

Some companies have experimented with an idea that owes much to military experience. They have attempted to create an executive decision making room, in which relevant data can be made available to the executives. Audio/visual techniques, large screen TV monitors, graphic plotters and other devices accessing information systems have all been tried.

In some cases success has been claimed, particularly when the executives are concerned with on-going operating decisions, such as the day to day running of an airline. Among the benefits claimed have been the co-ordination of effort, the improved staff work and a better basis for communication.

In other cases, to quote a Californian executive, 'it has been a horrible waste of time and money'. Where the decisions involve longer term managerial and strategic decisions, the decision room information systems can only provide a small part of the relevant data and frustrating delays can occur. Much depends on the type of decision and the style of the decision makers. Computer and telecommunication assisted information systems provided on-line to a decision room can facilitate discussions but are un-likely to be the principle sources of information, except for operating level decisions—for example, in the control of trains in a railroad system, air traffic control or control of an automated plant.

Information Centres

Another idea, of wider applicability, is the information centre, in which people, who know the contents of the data-bases and how to access them, provide an inter-face with the users. As the scale and detail of corporate data banks expands, so it becomes more necessary to offer potential users the services of an expert in the available data—just as a librarian plays a vital role in the modern library. Indeed the two roles are converging.

We will consider further the role and responsibilities of the data-base administrator in chapter 8.

On the Ownership of Information

As we have seen, the provision of data, however pro-fessional, achieves nothing unless someone uses it to become better informed. Data has a cost: it must be transformed into information to acquire value.

Consequently user involvement and commitment is of primary importance in developing information systems. The hallmark of success in the implementation of a system is when a user refers to 'my system' and 'my information', rather than 'their system' and 'their information'.

- A large manufacturing company installed data-capture devices on the floor of the plant. Operators were required to key in details of completed jobs. Error rates were high. Work in process information, which depended on this data, became inaccurate. Inventory records were incorrect, and management decided to revert to the previous manual record kept by the supervisors.

  The operators had no incentive to key in accurate data. As far as they were concerned it was a system designed by 'them' to keep a watch on 'us'.

  Some time later the company reintroduced the system, after they had created joint design teams. The new system, however, provides the operator with data of relevance to his work station—performance levels, work in hand, effect on pay incentives and so on. Now the operators refer to 'my' information. The potential conflict, when people are asked to collect and process data for higher management, when they have a personal stake in the data as well, was resolved.

  The people who are less pleased now are the supervisors, who, traditionally, had been the channels of communication from shop floor to management.

As we shall study further in the next chapter, the potential at the technical level and opportunities at the data management level provide management with fascinating issues at the organisational level.

- Telephone operators in a Scandinavian insurance company used to take messages about changes in policies and premiums from policy holders, and pass them on, in handwritten form, to the insurance clerks. Then the telephonists were given screens on-line to the company's files of policies and policy holders. They were able to relate to the customers in a new way, discussing with them the items on the file. They asked management if the files could be divided and each telephonist given responsibility for a specific set of customers. Management received many comments about the better, more helpful service, that the telephonists were providing.

Recently the telephonists approached management again and asked for access to the company's claims records, so that they could give an even better service to 'their' customers when they asked about the processing of claims. However, management are now unsure whether to accede to their request. They are hearing complaints from the insurance clerks, who feel their job is being eroded.

There are few limits at the technical or data management levels to the provision of terminal access to files. Increasingly, too, such applications are becoming cost-effective. Desk top equipment or a portable device for use over the public telephone lines can link the user into any files that are to be opened to him. Furthermore he can be provided with computational facilities, the opportunity to create his own files and to communicate with other users. The proverbial 'little black book' of the manager will have been computerised!

Whether he is a shop floor operator, a clerk, a middle manager or a top executive, the opportunities can be made available to provide access to data.

- An outside, independent director of a large public company has asked whether he may have a terminal to access the company files from his own home. In this way, he argues, he will not have to read so many board documents prior to meetings, but can search for answers to the question *he* thinks might be important.

The important implications lie at the organisational level. Obtaining answers is relatively easy: the real difficulty lies in understanding the questions.

Reference

1. *The President and information management: an experiment in the Carter White House*: Jon A. Turner and John A. Gosden: Center for Research on Information Systems; New York University/CRIS 12 GBA 80/119(CR) 1980.

6
An Organisational Perspective
•*new options in strategy, structure and style*

'Communication and community have common roots.'

Henry Boettinger

'Organisations are processes, not palaces.'

Bo Hedburg

'Information has a narcotic effect. It can lead to an addiction to computerisation. Every bit of information gives rise to a demand for more. We must improve our ability to identify information needs: not just improve our technology of handling data.'

Bob Gifford, Los Angeles Water & Power Department

In this chapter we consider the organisational level of information systems—the third and final level in the information system structure.

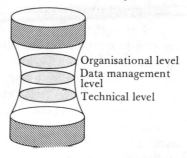

Organisational level
Data management level
Technical level

(a)

The Intelligent Organisation

When messages from a remote station had to be carried in a cleft stick by runners, and thence borne to Head Office by sailing ship, in the distant days of the great trading corporations, many weeks would pass between communications. Appropriate forms of organisation and managerial authority had to be developed.

Today with reliable data, text, voice and visual communications and computing becoming widely available and cost effective, managements face many more options in structuring their organisations. There are more choices in allocating decision making responsibilities. For example, senior executives may draw authority for some aspects of the business back towards the centre, as they are able to exercise greater corporate control overall: or they may push autonomy further out towards the periphery of the organisation, gaining greater involvement, local participation and motivation, whilst seeking more of a co-ordinating role at the centre.

There is a close parallel between information and organisation. After all, what is an organisation but a network of relationships kept alive by communications? It is not surprising, therefore, that information systems have an organisational dimension. Too great a concentration at the technical or data management levels of information systems can obscure the real significance at the organisational level. Managements can now choose how they want to run their business. Organisational adaptation need no longer be a response to crisis, but a planned shift towards alternatives that were previously unavailable or, even, unimaginable. But what *is* the relationship between organisation and information system?

The Impact of Information Systems

For over twenty years various experts have been speculating on the impact of information systems on organisation. In the early stages Leavitt & Whistler(1) forecast that middle management would become highly structured, top management more able to control directly, and there would be an end to inter-departmental conflicts. Dearden(2), in 1965, predicted that computers would have no effect on middle or top management, such effects being limited to operational control. In 1970 Hefer(3) observed few effects on the formal structure of organisations and Stewart(4) in 1971 reported from her studies that there was little observable structural effect, but that computers placed greater demands for discipline and tight time schedules on those providing the basic data and that there were fewer opportunities in computerised systems for human intervention to correct problems.

Given this sort of experience some system experts insist that information systems are totally independent of organisation and can be built to meet specific data needs. But others are less sure. It does seem that information systems take on some of the characteristics of the organisation.

Just consider the following very short descriptions of four different information systems. What do they also tell us about the four organisations?

- The first system has linked processors on either side of the Atlantic, with terminals on-line in various plant locations in Europe and North America. The main application is logistics control with production scheduling, parts inventories and supply. Much systems effort goes into teleprocessing and communications control to keep the system on the air.

- The second system has computers from four mainframe manufacturers spread around nearly 100 installations on four continents. There is no teleprocessing or remote access of any significance. Each of the systems stand alone and undertakes a variety of different applications, although some of the configurations are quite complex and the installations large. Most of the application programmes are transaction based. There is a Head Office advisory systems team, but there are no common programmes. Mini computers are increasingly being used in some locations.

- The third system is on a single site. It has visual display units throughout the organisation. Files are mainly related to people. The system's basic use is information retrieval. The system is operational around the clock, reliability has a high emphasis and limited access is ensured by priority and security checks.

- The final example is of a very large data-base, containing personnel records in great detail. Updating can be input from remote locations as well as from central inputs. There is a strong emphasis on security, including the duplication of files in separate locations.

Even from these extremely brief thumbnail sketches, it is possible to deduce much about each organisation, its nature, structure and style. For example, the first organisation must have centrally co-ordinated manufacturing and, therefore, is likely to be an integrated operation manufacturing standard items in various locations. If you went on to guess the motor industry you would be right.

By contrast the second example, also of an international organisation, can be deduced to have relatively autonomous remote divisions, with little intertrading. Divisional managers will have significant degrees of freedom.

The third example is of patient recording in a hospital and the last of the records of one of the armed services. Students experienced in systems work can build up a surprisingly realistic picture of an organisation from descriptions of its information systems alone, even down to management style and organisational climate.

Or is it so surprising? Surely it is intuitively obvious that scale and location, technology, organisation structure and management style each affect the decisions in an enterprise, and, consequently, the needs for information. At one level of abstraction this opinion seems irrefutable; but in operational terms it does not relate to the shape of the information system. To say that information systems must reflect the organisation's situation and needs is one thing; to say they must mirror them is quite another. Is it not possible to have a relatively decentralised organisation structure with heavily centralised information systems? As one systems director put it 'the plumbing has nothing to do with organisation'.

In fact the question about the dependence or independence of information systems on organisation is irrelevant. The reality is that they are interdependent. There is no need for a common configuration: a centralised technical level computing does not necessitate a centralised organisation, or vice versa. But information systems and organisation may not be treated in isolation—changes in one will have impacts on the other. Change the organisation and demands on the information system will change.

- AT & T, the American Telephone and Telegraph Company changed its organisation from a functional grouping emphasising service to product streams emphasising profit. Many of the information systems had to be redesigned completely to collect and drive the data in quite different directions.

Moreover, changes at the technical and data management levels of information systems can have a direct impact on organisation.

- A bank computerised the local branch operations, automating much of the 'teller' cashier's work. What they discovered was that the manager's job had also changed. Once the centre of the local business community, running his own office and maintaining the accounts of his customers; he now complained of being made a 'salesman' for Head Office services, with accounting and control over his customers centralised. 'It's no longer the same bank', he said.

Management can now plan its organisational developments in relation to its information system developments and vice versa. That is why the model of information systems, we have adopted, has the third, organisational level.

The researchers, seeking the impact of computers on organisation, had the wrong question. The issue is the extent of the interdependence. But if the technical level is not to dictate the direction of the business, which would be the equivalent of the ship's engine room giving instructions to the bridge on the course to be steered, we must start with strategy. Information system developments should stem from business needs not the desire to use computers and communication systems more effectively.

On Strategy, Structure and Style

It used to be argued(5) that, for effective management, organisation structure should follow the formulation of strategy, just as modern architects have been advised that form should follow function. There is an intuitive logic in this proposition. First of all determine what is to be done and then put the organisation in place to do it.

However, in the large, complex enterprise it may not be that simple. Organisations can take a long time to adapt and changes can be expensive; attitudes can take even longer to change. The organisation structure and management style of an organisation can have an effect on the formulation of strategy. Consequently we need to consider all three, and their inter-relationships:

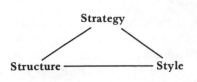

The formulation of strategy involves strategic assessment, choice and implementation. It is the way the policy makers chart the way ahead for the enterprise. Strategic assessment is a process of scanning the external environment, identifying and appreciating the issues, opportunities and threats facing the enterprise; understanding the strengths and weaknesses in the resources available to the organisation; and overall determining the mission and the goals of the business. Strategic choice involves the development of alternative strategies—different paths the business might take, through diversification, acquisition, new products, investment, or research, for example, evaluating their strengths and weaknesses and coming to a decision about strategies that can then form the basis for planning and implementing in detail.

Organisation structure can be viewed in various ways. The classical picture is of the *command structure*—the formal organisational boundaries and shape. The organisation chart portrays this picture of who reports to whom, with responsibility and commensurate authority delegated downwards and accountability required upwards. Despite its traditional, military roots, this model of organisation remains fundamental to the practice of management control today, although re-evaluation is occurring in matrix and task group organisation forms. Structure is necessary to enable complex tasks to be completed: but it can promote organisational inertia or encourage change depending on its nature.

Secondly an organisation can be perceived in terms of its *political structure*, that is as a coalition of differing interests, often in competition and, perhaps, conflict. There is a tendency in political structures to reduce complexity in decision making: clearly communication is a major factor.

But, basically, organisation is about relationships. It is a means of reflecting the perceptions of the organisational members of their roles and positions vis a vis each other. Information and decisions are primary to this view of organisation as an *information structure*.

In studying the structure of an organisation two different dimensions can be useful. Firstly *configuration*, or the shape and relationships between the component parts—

In the entrepreneurial organisation the structure will be dominated by, and revolve around, the entrepreneur. The functional organisation is grouped by departmental tasks— purchasing, manufacturing, sales, accounts, design etc. The divisionalised organisation is divided into separate entities for performance by product group, market or geographical location, for example.

The second dimension is *the degree of centralisation*—how much power and authority is vested in the organisational parts. Many executives talk in terms of centralisation and decentralisation, imagining a scale along which they can move their organisation. But thinking only in terms of geographical locations or organisational boundaries can be naive. The concept is rather more subtle, with various aspects, for example:-

- Dependence—The level of dependence on central authority in decision making. At what stage managers refer to higher authority. The prescribed or perceived boundaries of discretion.

- Formalisation—The extent of written rules and formal information channels, the existence of standard procedures.

- Identification—The degree of commitment to unit goals, leading to potential suboptimisation, against identification with the overall objectives of the whole organisation, leading to possible synergies.

- Influence—The relative importance perceived by others. The key position in the work flow or provision of scarce, expert knowledge.

- Accountability—Determining who is accountable for the exercise of authority: the methods of defining and measuring performance. Ideas of efficiency, productivity, competence. Emphasis on stewardship. Existence of targets, budgets, standards and other performance measures. Reporting requirements.

- Enforcement—The extent of the pressure for performance and the methods used to activate and require accountability; encouragement and exhortation; rewards both monetary and in status, position, privileges; regulation by rule or law; sanctions such as monetary penalisation or loss of status, position or privileges; punishment.

Configuration and the degree of centralisation are both important aspects in understanding organisation structure. They bring together the formal, command structure and the political structure. Information system changes can affect many of those elements of structure.

Management Style is an elusive, but important, idea that describes the way the organisation is managed. Let us consider some contrasting styles.

Autocracy. In the early stages, commercial enterprises tend to be dominated by individuals. They start the business and they run it. They make the decisions and their image is stamped throughout. It is their company.

In the late 19th and early 20th centuries these were the men who gave their names to companies that were to become institutions—Henry Ford, Alfred Herbert, Krupps, William Morris, Westinghouse, Woolworth. Not that such management styles are things of the past. Jack Cohen built up Tesco supermarkets in the 1950s and 1960s with his dictum 'Pile it high and sell it cheap'. Robert Maxwell with Pergamon Press and 'Tiny' Rowlands with Lonhro have created significant companies in the 1960s and 1970s, which they still dominate, much to the chagrin of the financial institutions.

More recently Freddie Laker has forged ahead with Laker Airways, completely changing the trans-Atlantic fare structure in the process. Silicon chip technology and the development of systems software are also providing new opportunities for entrepreneurially inclined individuals.

Such businessmen tend to be autocrats. This is the entrepreneurial style, much vaunted by business for an apparent freedom to act and take initiatives. Some people speak of autocratic management solely in pejorative terms. They miss an important point. Such businessmen often show a paternal concern for their employees—and their employees respond to that commitment with loyalty towards them—which is strikingly different from the coolly, cost-beneficial attitudes struck by some self-styled professional managers.

In terms of information and information systems, the dominant, autocratic individual tends to be his own information system. He wants to be personally in touch with the people and the events that affect his enterprise. Not for him the remote report and the arms-length management style. Personal involvement, not committees, is his approach. Of course, he recognises that records, accounts and routine controls are necessary, not least for the auditor and tax authority. But the entrepreneur tends to have little time for the formal organisation or an extensive MIS. He wants the flexibility, ready response and inside knowledge that stems from personal involvement. In the end it can be his undoing.

Let us create a quadrant (fig. 6/1) to show the focus of attention of different executives, and their related sources of information. We can distinguish those with the external, environmental view from those with the alternative internal orientation—on the horizontal axis. On the vertical axis we distinguish those whose approach to information is formal and systematic from those with an ad hoc and unsystematic approach. Our entrepreneurial autocrat is fundamentally externally orientated and idiosyncratic. He is in the bottom right hand quadrant.

Systematic & routine approach		
Unsystematic & ad hoc requirements		The entrepreneurial autocrat's orientation
	Internal view	External view

Figure 6/1. The Focus of Managerial Information

Bureaucracy. As organisations grow they inevitably become more complex. Each additional node in a communication network (for example, an additional person or an extra department) adds in arithmetical progression to the number of information channels.

Number of Nodes	Number of Channels
1	0
2	1
3	3
4	6
5	10
10	45
20	190
100	4,950
1,000	495,000

In expanding organisation formal procedures, policies and rules are soon required to regulate the information channels. If the enterprise is to remain stable, coherent and co-ordinated formal systems for information and control become necessary.

A bureaucracy emerges. Again the term has a pejorative ring. Bureaucratic excesses, just like autocratic extremes, have brought concepts into disrepute. But we should recognise bureaucracy as a coherent style of management administration.

Public sector organisations—hospitals, police forces, the military, local authorities, government departments—denied the entrepreneurial innovator, tend to slip into a bureaucratic style from the outset. The emphasis is on effective administration, rather than strategic management. The public service is no place for the entrepreneur; the exercise of power is a political process; the interests of different interest groups have to be recognised, and patterns of responsibility and accountability differ.

- Officials of the California State Government, reporting on the use of data processing in the State wrote:

  'The problems were made intractable by the special constraints suffered in a State environment; for example, the separation of powers and the relationships between the elected members, the appointed members, the civil service and contract staff.

Interdependence and independence in units of government put limitations on exchange of information.'

On the information quadrant, the bureaucrat is clearly orientated toward the internal and the systematic view (fig. 6/2).

Not surprisingly, since the bureaucrat grew up in the commercial organisation as a counter to the autonomy of the entrepreneur, or in the public sector to avoid domination by individuals or interest groups, we find the bureaucratic orientation to be diametrically opposite to that of the autocratic entrepreneur. Here we meet the organisation man. We also find very necessary management control systems.

Systematic & routine approach	The bureaucrats' information orientation	
Unsystematic & ad hoc requirements		
	Internal view	External view

Figure 6/2. The Focus of Managerial Information

Meritocracy.   Throughout the 1950s, 1960s and early 1970s various schools of professional management tended to influence management thinking.

Sloan, at General Motors, moved ideas beyond the functional (and bureaucratic) organisation, with departmental responsibilities for production, sales, finance etc. to a concept of managerial decentralisation. Competing, semi-autonomous divisions were created to be profit responsible, with central oversight of pricing and performance.

Cordinair, at General Electric, sharpened the decentralised approach with his emphasis on divisional performance measures. Management by objectives, management by exception and similar concepts reinforced the professionalisation of management. Drucker, who described the Sloan work, became an influential exponent of the professional practice of management.

In the meantime, as Berle & Means(6) showed, management

tended to become divorced from the owners of capital. A professional, managerial meritocracy emerged, Burnham(7). Now the prerogative to manage stemmed not from a founder's privilege, the rights of ownership or a bureaucratic appointment, but from professional competence.

The focus on information is still, predominantly, in the top left quadrant—internal and systematic. This is the world of management accounting, cost controls, budgets, return on investment calculations and quantitative performance measures. The accountant has a major role to play. But increasingly interest pushes out for information about the external environment and ad hoc reports on internal matters.

The Changing Managerial Situation

The world of Henry Ford, like that of all entrepreneurs, is a relatively simple place. Facing a significant strategic decision— for example, to launch a new product, open new facilities, change the technology, alter the capital structure—the entrepreneur has to monitor his external environment for himself.

The mental sketchmap of an entrepreneur (fig. 6/3) as we saw in chapter 2 probably has little more in focus than the business itself, its sources of finance, suppliers of goods and services, the customers and the competitors.

Figure 6/3. An Entrepreneur's Mental Map.

By contrast the modern executive perceives a world that is infinitely more complex and volatile. He sees an infinity of external entities (fig. 6/4) which offer potential information for his decisions. Beyond them he recognises a changing external situation—economic, technological, social, political, legal, commercial and international, all of which affect his perceptions.

The information horizons of the modern executive need to be wider and further than those of the entrepreneur or the

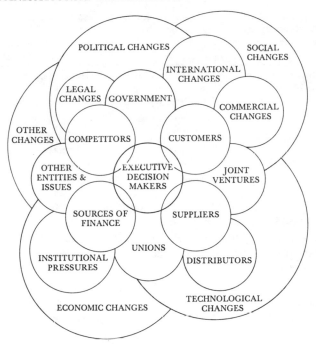

Figure 6/4. The Modern Executive's Mental Map

bureaucrat. He interacts with information systems to widen his information horizons. Nor is the problem confined to the business. A similar mental map can be drawn for the administrator of a modern public sector organisation. His external environment, too, has become volatile and complex. Referenda, city meetings, interest and lobby groups all add new demands for access to information and participation in decision making.

Putting the Entrepreneur Back Into Enterprise

Under pressures from turbulent conditions and economic constraints, there is a tendency in the modern organisation to concentrate on internally generated information. When times are difficult, orders scarce, cash short, attention is given to those systems in the top left hand quadrant. In reality the needs may be for information about the external and uncertain environment in the opposite sector.

Systematic & routine		Access to data bases containing environmental data
Unsystematic & ad hoc requirements	'Need' related data-bases— facilitating search by the user	Decision-support systems
	Internal view	External view

Figure 6/5. Potential focus of Managerial Information

The technology is now available to provide access to data about many aspects of an organisation's external environment in the top right quadrant. As we have seen such data-bases may be maintained internally or access may be provided to externally available files.

Now the manager can question and search for his own information needs. No longer does the systems analyst have to predetermine the information that he feels the decision maker will need.

The potential for responding to unsystematic and ad hoc information requirements on aspects of the internal position in the organisation in the lower left quadrant also exists. Technology is available to facilitate searches by a user on a 'needs related' approach.

Finally, in the bottom right hand quadrant we have seen the growing potential to respond in an ad hoc way to a decision maker's needs for information. In this way we may be able to reintroduce entrepreneurial abilities into the large organisation.

The shift from the upper left hand quadrant to the other quadrants represents the challenge of the modern information system. In effect the potential is now available to move beyond large, formal and internal systems emphasising the processing of the organisation's routine transactions, to systems which facilitate access to real information.

Organisational Alternatives

There are no panaceas in organisational design; no correct solutions to the problem of determining appropriate configurations, degrees of centralisation or management styles; just some approaches that may give better results under some conditions.

The search for the right balance between centralised control and decentralised autonomy is not new. At least it is the issue that has fascinated philosophies for centuries—the equating of order with freedom.

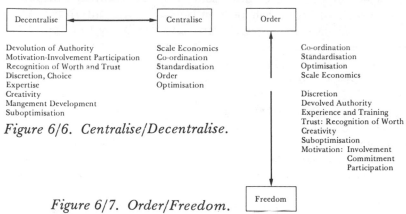

Figure 6/6. Centralise/Decentralise.

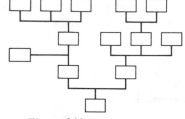

Figure 6/7. Order/Freedom.

Today the designer of the latter-day equivalent of Plato's Greek city states—the modern enterprise—has more opportunities for handling communication and information. The potential at the technical and data management levels open up a vista of organisational alternatives. There are choices in structure and style.

Organisations inevitably have limited information processing facilities, and standard procedures and controls provide consistency and conserve energy. This is fine for stable conditions and predictable futures. Clerical and early computer methods tended to reinforce the classical command structure, with hierarchical accountability.

Such approaches can produce organisational inertia and an inability to adapt sufficiently

Figure 6/8

fast to threats, particularly if success in the past has reinforced the traditional attitudes. Traditional information systems can make organisations rigid and inflexible, filtering out the very signals that warn of necessary change. This is the mark of the obsolete organisation.

 ˙But information systems can offer multiple reporting and multi-directional controls. They can also facilitate self-management and the creative search for alternatives. Different structures and styles can be combined in one enterprise. The stability to withstand pressure and the flexibility to respond to rapidly emerging opportunities or threats can be combined.

The transient organisation is a viable model for the future—able to adapt constantly, yet with sufficient stability to achieve results. Matrix organisations, in which project teams were mapped across functional departments, were a response to the demands of aerospace programmes for organisations that could cope with complexity and change. The traditional hierarchy of functional control was too cumbersome to put a man on the moon within two years. The matrix idea has been adapted for

	Functional Departments			
Project 1	x	x		
2		x		
3			x	
4	x			x

Figure 6/9

use in marketing orientated companies, with product managers responsibilities for product/market performance cutting across the hierarchy of functional responsibilities; and, increasingly in large multinationals with product streams cutting across regional companies.

	USA	Europe	Australasia
Oil			
Petrochemicals			
Coal			
Nuclear			
Transportation			
Retailing			

Figure 6/10

In a major oil company the manager of operations in, say, Germany, might find himself reporting both to his regional boss and to his product group manager.

Task forces and project groups, formed to achieve specific purposes and with a limited life are likely to be a feature of modern organisations as they respond to the challenges of change. Such organisation work teams can operate alongside a more mechanistic structure, designed to achieve profits from existing opportunities.

What is vital is an information system that is responsive to the organisational demands placed on it. Nor are the issues confined to the enterprise itself.

Boundless Businesses

An unexpected effect of technical and data management level developments in information systems has been to change the boundaries of the enterprise itself.

- A bank has installed terminals in a retailer's stores. Customers may now transact business with the bank from these remote locations. If the bank goes further and enables the retailer to debit the customer's account directly where does the boundary lie? Is the bank involved in the retailer's business or has the retailer assumed part of the banking responsibility?

Interconnections between the enterprise and other organisations have multiplied rapidly—between banker and customer, supplier and customer, manufacturer and wholesaler, insurance company and agent, corporation and government department . . . The boundaries of the modern organisation are, themselves, increasingly transient and flexible. Data management and technical level systems offer the key.

In the future joint ventures between companies, short-term associations with government departments, co-operative links between manufacturers and so on are likely to become vital—as the cost of entry, basic research and design and capital investment in many mature industries and markets become prohibitive for a single company.

Information system boundaries, in the future, may not be those dictated solely by the company.

Increasing Organisational Intelligence

Actually, what the modern organisation needs is not more information per se but better informed people. We have seen how information involves the user, the data available to him and his organisational situation. It is apparent, therefore, that management development, information system development and organisational development are closely related. Although in most enterprises they are currently managed quite separately in different departments, there is a case for much closer liaison and commonality.

We have seen how strategy, structure and style are interrelated and all affected by information systems in the enterprise. Management needs to manage this interaction.

Unfortunately in some organisations there tends to be a generation gap, or two, as top executives, enthusiastic and committed to high technology and the use of modern computing and telecommunications, fail to recognise the social and cultural implications. Ideas developed early in their managerial experience, and reinforced by decades of success, are more difficult to adapt. Continuing education and attitudinal change are vital: and that, in effect, is what a modern information system does to an organisation—turns it into a learning system—able to react and adapt to change; flexible and reliable to perform well, yet rugged enough to survive.

References

1. Leavitt & Whistler: *Harvard Business Review*: Nov/Dec. 1958.
2. Dearden: *Harvard Business Review*: March/April 1965.
3. Hofer: *Harvard Business Review*: March/April 1970.
4. Stewart, R.: *How computers affect management*: Macmillan, 1971.
5. Chandler, A. D.: *Strategy & structure*: MIT, 1962.
6. Berle, A. A. and B. C. Means: *The modern corporation and private property*: Harcourt, Brace & World, 1932. Revised 1968.
7. Burnham J.: *The managerial revolution*: Penguin 1941 and 1962.

7
Developing an Information Systems Strategy
•systems planning as part of corporate strategy

'Our systems seem set like concrete. It's difficult now to respond quickly enough to business needs.'
Chief Executive, Australian Insurance Company

'We have good systems and lots of data: but we don't seem to have good information. How *do* you get top management concerned?'
Data Processing Manager, South African Company

'Most managements today get involved in their systems. But that's not enough. They need commitment. It's like eggs and bacon. The hen is involved: but you can believe the pig is committed.'
Director I.S. UK Company

In the earlier chapters we have seen that, whereas data-processing and computing used to provide support for the basic operations of an enterprise, they now play a fundamental role in organisations. There are implications for strategy, structure and style. It is no longer enough for top management to be enthusiastic and supportive: there are issues at their level to decide.

How can such a strategic focus be given to the development of information systems? That is the topic for this chapter.

Bottom Up or Top Down?

Many approaches to the planning and management of computer-based systems have been tried over the years.

In the early stages, when applications are well bounded and relatively insignificant to the organisation as a whole, there may be little call for a corporate systems plan. This approach (often referred to as the 'bottom-up' approach), enables departments and other organisational units to introduce equipment and applications piecemeal when the need or the opportunity arises. It is argued, in justification, that making an integrated corporate-wide systems plan is too difficult; and, moreover, that it is unnecessary because success is more likely when each part of the business is motivated to find its own solutions to data processing.

By contrast, the advocates of a 'top-down' approach see the dangers in random, piecemeal developments—lack of co-ordination, little standardisation, loss of scale economies, no integration of data flows, 'reinvention of the wheel' in different departments and suboptimisation as separate units take decisions which are beneficial to the achievement of their own, shorter-term, goals but detrimental to the organisation as a whole.

The 'top-down' approach calls for the investment in an overall plan for systems developments, so that each proposed application and every acquisition of equipment will be consistent with the grand design.

The obvious disadvantage of the overall systems plan is that corporate situations, and thus system requirements, can change fundamentally. In turbulent times companies may divest or acquire major units, enter or leave markets or entire business sectors, contract or expand with alacrity. Moreover system technology and electronic hardware themselves are constantly developing.

- An American bank, having invested heavily and restructured its organisation around a centralised information system, now wonders whether it would have been better to have more intelligent terminals at each branch enabling them to run their own part of the business.

The key danger of the overall systems plan is the creation of an information-handling, nervous system for an industrial dinosaur. The problem of not having one is the threat of expensive data-processing anarchy.

What we need is a process that will enable top management to set, and to change, the broad directions for systems development and the management of the data resource in line with the

evolving corporate, strategic needs. A case example of the way
one organisation has moved in this direction will be illuminating.

- An English local authority, responsible for the administration of one of the country's largest urban
  conurbations, had been a major user of data-processing
  for many years.

  In 1974 a need was felt to improve the planning and
  control for DP developments, provide appropriate
  central facilities and to co-ordinate and integrate computing services. Accordingly a small central unit was
  created, under the control of a newly appointed Head
  of Data Processing. His responsibilities included the
  approval of all DP expenditure and system developments, the provision of central computer services and
  support staff, and the oversight of each department's
  use of computers to ensure efficient and economic
  operations.

  By 1977 the Head of DP had been re-named the Head
  of Computing Services, reporting to the Chief Finance
  Officer of the Council. But some problems were being
  experienced with the service-orientated, centrally
  located computing service, which by this time had
  become a large installation. They had to react to
  demands from the different departments for disparate
  applications and widely different types of data.
  Demands were increasing month by month, and all
  that the Central Services could do was to react by
  expanding. There were inevitable delays in responding to this complicated and unco-ordinated set of
  demands. Users were voicing some frustrations.

  The alternative of abandoning Central Services and
  reorganising computing into smaller, relatively independent departmental units, was considered.
  Various potential benefits were recognised. Priorities
  would be determined by the departmental management concerned. Systems development would be
  simpler, with close user involvement. Some economies

might be achieved; although staff costs were expected to rise and scale economies would be lost.

In the event the Council decided to adopt a combination of central and more local facilities. Computers were to be located both within departments and centrally. The Head of Computing Services was given the task of overall planning and controlling information system developments.

By planning developments, a wider range of options could be considered by the Central Service. Greater efficiency and effectiveness could be achieved by balancing central and local efforts. User involvement would be secured, whilst the duplication of effort through the departments and the incompatibilities between systems, data standards and equipment could be avoided.

This central responsibility with local autonomy has paved the way for significant changes that were subsequently brought about by the changing economic climate and changes in the political persuasion of the Council.

This approach, combining many of the benefits of both the 'bottom up' and the 'top-down' approaches, can be thought of as a strategic approach to information systems.

A Strategic Approach

Information systems strategy needs to be a component of the overall, longer term strategic thinking of the enterprise. It is closely related to strategies on manpower, management and organisational development. It needs to be considered alongside, and not merely as a support to, strategies for products and markets, finance, investment, acquisition or divestment. The information system strategy can have direct impacts on the other elements in the corporate strategy and significantly affect overall corporate performance.

Definition: Information Systems Strategy is a component of the overall strategic thinking in an organisation, by which top management determine their longer term needs for investment in computing and communications, the management of the data resource and the development of organisation structure and management style, in line with the mission of the enterprise and in the light of available resources and recognising the strategic issues and opportunities facing the enterprise.

Consequently an information systems strategy is more than a plan for computing developments. It requires a strategic focus. Opportunities in computing and communications can lead the way to other strategic developments in markets, finance, production and the other sectors of the corporate strategies. A case example may emphasise the significance.

- The Prescription Pricing Authority is part of the British National Health Service. Its primary function is to calculate the sums due to chemists for drugs and dispensing services provided to patients under the Health Service.

  Chemists had been complaining at delays in reimbursement and an outside consultant was invited to report(1). The problem was conceived initially in terms of improving the data-processing capability of the PPA.

  The system in focus, initially consisted of the nation's chemists, who sent some 50 million prescription forms each year after they had been dispensed to the PPA where they were priced, calculated and the sums due notified to the local Family Practitioner Committee for reimbursement. Viz:

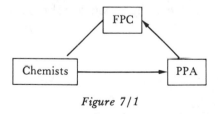

Figure 7/1

  Certainly the chemists problems could have been addressed at such a tactical level, and various remedies proposed. However, it became apparent during the study that more was involved. It was the doctor who wrote the prescription before giving it to the patient to take to the chemist. Perhaps the doctor, or the chemist could be persuaded to undertake some pricing or coding to facilitate the work of the many clerks in the PPA?

Representatives of the doctors provided evidence that caused concern. Patients were increasingly demanding a right to drugs for every conceivable malady including their own social incapabilities. Moreover they expressed the hope that nothing done to improve administrative effectiveness would reduce their own right to prescribe what they liked, in whatever quantities they liked, as they thought appropriate.

The system had now taken on socio-medical and ethical dimensions:

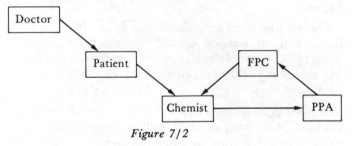

Figure 7/2

The Department of Health, with the Treasury behind them, wanted to use the data within the PPA to build some controls on prescribing and drug expenditure into the system. Now there was a political as well as an economic dimension:

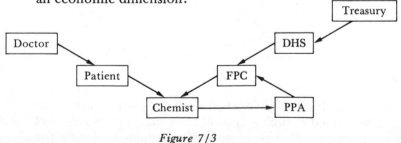

Figure 7/3

Finally it became apparent that a cornerstone of the primary pharmaceutical service was the drug companies which supplied the chemists. Without a commercial market place for their products in the UK, prices were negotiated with the DHSS. But the drug companies promoted their drugs vigorously to the doctors. Now there were fundamental issues in the picture, with economic, political, social, medical, commercial and ethical dimensions:

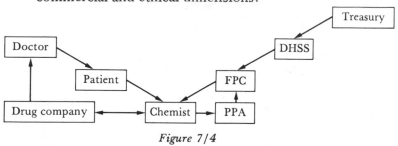

Figure 7/4

What had begun as a study into the data-processing efficiency of the PPA, was now seen to involve a strategically important system. The PPA had the potential to provide an information system relevant to the medical profession, the government, the drug industry, the chemists and to medical research.

The Process of Strategy Formulation

Before we consider the development of information system strategies, it will be worth while to reflect briefly on the process of strategy formulation generally. Conceptually there is little difference between the two.

Every enterprise has its strategies. They may be the unarticulated, random, inspirational thoughts of a charismatic leader, an autocratic entrepreneur or a powerful politician: or they may be the result of careful analysis and detailed planning by a chairman and his board, after much deliberation by the executives and staff work by corporate planners. The essential elements are the same—strategic assessment, choice and implementation—although the extent of the professional effort may differ greatly.

Strategic assessment is the process of understanding the strategic situation facing the enterprise. It has three aspects—reviewing the mission and objectives, recognising the external issues, threats and opportunities and identifying the strengths and weaknesses of the resources available.

Figure 7/5

Reviewing the mission and the objectives of an enterprise means bringing into focus its real purposes. We are not talking about bland, public relations statements on fair dealings with customers, good conditions for employees or reasonable dividends for shareholders. This review is to understand the forces that really provide the drive to the enterprise: the sum total of what people are trying to achieve, what those at the top believe the enterprise is set to do.

Constraints, threats and opportunities from the external environment face every enterprise. Scanning the competitive, economic, technological, governmental, political, international, commercial, social, financial and other relevant circumstances provides the basis for such an external assessment. Short term data provides the information for the updating of the longer term strategic expectations.

Then there is need to identify the strengths and weakness of the internal resources—building on the one and reducing the other. Availability of skilled labour, professional management, technical know-how, market standing, credit worthiness and so on must all be seen in their strategic context.

The interplay between mission, external circumstances and internal strengths and weaknesses leads to the strategic assessment—a longer term view of the situation and potential to achieve desired results.

Strategic choice is a process of formulating alternative strategies from the information generated in the strategic assessment, evaluating those alternatives and making choices about strategic directions to follow.

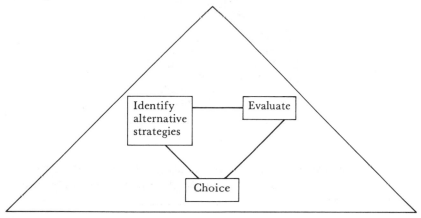

Figure 7/6

A business may face many strategic alternatives—new product and market directions, further investment in major research and development, investment in new production technologies, retrenchment and the closing of production plants, acquisitions, divestments, international restructuring, financial alternatives— but longer term internal resources and external circumstances necessitate choices.

Implementation of strategy calls for the development of plans that can carry the strategy into being. Without action any strategy is no more than an intent.

On the one hand action planning requires the development of policies that provide guidelines for management (for example on the approvals required for specific investments) and the creation of procedures (for example on the control of system development activities). Without policies and procedures, middle management will have no rules or regulations to channel their actions in line with the strategic intent. On the other hand plans must be broken down into operational elements through sets of programmes and specific projects so that they are of a manageable size. Budgets relevant to each project in a programme also need to be developed, giving both the resources allocated, the expenditure expected and the time dimensions involved.

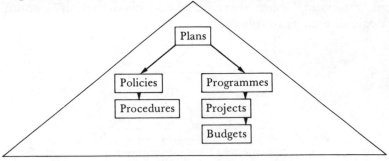

Figure 7/7

These three elements of strategic assessment, strategic choice and implementation constitute the process of strategy formulation:

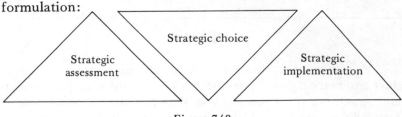

Figure 7/8

It will be apparent that the strategic position emerging from the final stage is, in effect, today's strategy that forms the basis for strategic changes in the future.

Developing an Information Systems Strategy

Since the formulation of information systems strategy is part of the overall strategy formulation, it follows that the same elements of the strategy formulation process will also apply. The development of information systems now represent a significant investment for many organisations, with a long term commitment. Consequently it is worth while considering how each of the various elements can be pursued in practice. Viz:

Review of the mission and objectives

Recognition of external issues, threats and opportunities

Identification of strengths and weaknesses of the internal recourses

Identification of alternative strategies

Evaluation of alternatives

Choice

Implementation—Policies	Programmes
Procedures	Projects
	Budgets

Moreover, the strategic planning process for information systems needs to be integrated with the other sectors of an organisation's overall corporate plans. We must consider how this is to be achieved.

- A large oil company had a sophisticated long range plan for computer developments. Unfortunately it had been created in isolation from the product and market development plans, and was not updated in phase with changes in the business strategy. Eventually a crisis occurred when there was a fundamental shift in marketing policy. 'We are tending to revert to manual systems, to meet the urgent, rapid changes in data needs', the Chief Executive said.

In the last chapter we saw that, in every enterprise, strategy, structure and style are closely related. Consequently any approach to the formulation of information systems strategy must be consistent with the organisation structure and management style of the business—that is with the way it is organised and the way it goes about managing its activities. A pro-forma approach to the development of strategies is naive: there are no panaceas.

Nevertheless there is considerable experience that can be used. The research, from which this book draws its material, has studied the approaches of many different organisations and interviewed hundreds of executives.

In chapter 3 we identified various stages that an organisation might be in, as the organisation of its information systems, computing and communication develops. The formulation of strategy, obviously, will depend on the stage the company is at, and where responsibilities for systems development lie.

Stage 1 strategy.   In the early days of the introduction of computing and electronic equipment into office processes there is, typically, no longer term planning. Indeed there is often little planning at all. Developments are piecemeal, existing operations are replaced or supplemented, and there are few organisational implications.

- In 1981 an Oxford College introduced three word processing terminals with a printer into its office, to assist the text editing of Fellows' books and papers. There was no discussion of strategy, although some Fellows did reflect on the longer term potential for typing students' work, with them having access to the terminals, and also of being able to link the system directly to the systems of their publishers around the world, and perhaps accessing their work directly to scholarly librarians. The strategic implications were not considered.

Stage 2 strategy.   As user involvement grows and the information systems begin to straddle and to change organisational boundaries and processes, some planning begins to appear. The executive responsible for the systems work finds it necessary to draw up some overview of the system plans to determine where the focus of developments should be. Once users begin to make demands the 'ad-hocracy' of the early stages needs supplementing with some sort of look ahead. It is rare, at this stage, to find any attempt at longer term planning or strategy formulation.

Stages 3 and 4 strategy.   Once the data-processing or systems function is established the need for serious planning becomes apparent. Typically organisations have a major commitment to computing at this stage and their investment and expenditure have become significant.

Annual budgets become a necessity, with appropriate reporting of variances, as the basis for management control of annual expenditures. Investment appraisal for system projects are introduced, identifying the performance criteria that are to be satisfied.

Computing has become a professional endeavour at this stage, and the expertise is available to create a detailed and comprehensive plan for system developments. Such a plan may well have a time horizon of three to five years, and indicate the directions in which the information system will be extended in the years ahead. Less frequently such a plan may be supported with rolled-forward budget figures.

- A co-operative retail organisation in Canada developed a very professional plan for the extension and integration of its computer-based information system. They planned to link their check-out tills at each store with a central computer as the basis of immediate stock control, sales statistics and pricing/promotion policies.

  The plan did not anticipate the claim of the staff unions for upgrading the job of check-out assistants because their jobs had become more important. In the event this caused a long delay to the implementation of the system, and significantly changed its financial attractiveness.

Stage 5 strategy.   As data is recognised as a valuable corporate resource, to be managed by someone responsible for data administration, an additional element is added to the planning process. Budgets are needed for this new department; and costs and outputs of handling data are highlighted.

Moreover, the process of establishing data standards and a data dictionary tend to raise some basic questions about the nature and purpose of the enterprise. Management may be called on to determine some strategic issues.

- In developing a data-administration function, for the world-wide co-ordination of its information systems, a pharmaceutical company found that it had to make decisions about the production and marketing of certain drugs in different countries first. Previously,

When such choices arose unco-ordinated, ad hoc decisions were made by middle management. Now there had to be a policy which laid down precise rules for drugs that could be made and sold in each region.

Stage 6 strategy.   At this stage the 'user is king'. Now we find, really for the first time, the elements of long term, strategic thinking. Information system developments need to be set in the context of the strategic needs of the enterprise as whole.

Typically, at this stage, systems developments are significant and must be planned; the commitment to computing is large; and the annual cost is high. Usually an attempt is made to produce both short term (annual) plans for systems developments with budgets for computer operations and data administration, in line with a longer term (often 3-5 year) system plan.

A key question is now 'who takes the lead in determining the direction of systems developments—the user or the data processing function?' The emphasis on the user needs at this stage necessitates the integration of systems planning with overall corporate planning.

As one would expect, approaches differ in practice between companies; just as they differ on overall strategy, structure and style. In the next paragraphs we will review specific methods in practice. But first let us consider the last stage of development.

Stage 7 strategy.   At this stage organisations separate the information systems function from a new function responsible for the corporate communication and computing facilities. Specific responsibilities are identified for user management, the management of the information systems function and the management of computing and telecommunication equipment. The strategy formulation process must, obviously, reflect this separation of responsibility and the strategic interests of the various areas in the enterprise. Again we will see how this can be done by examining practical case examples.

The evolution of ideas on the development of systems is summarised in Table 1.

The Formulation of Information Systems Strategy in Practice

Table 1. *The Evolution of Ideas in Systems Development.*

Phase	Driving Force	Emphasis
'Bottom-up' planning	The DP function and the computer manufacturers	Transaction orientated systems to reduce costs & improve efficiency of operations. Information is an incidental result.
'Top-down' planning	Senior management and consultants	A response to crises in the 'Bottom-up' approach. Organisational effectiveness becomes important. Information needs are determined.
Systems evolution	Users of data and academic researchers	Systems evolve as organisations learn. The emphasis must be user orientated. Self-design is suggested.
Strategic development	Top management and professional communications people	The strategic implications of information systems too great & wide-spread to be treated other than as part of the corporate strategy formulation process.

1. Systems Planning in a Divisionalised Company with a Central MIS Function

A United States manufacturing company, with an annual turnover of about $1 billion, in capitally intensive engineering products, is organised into twenty separate divisions, each with management responsible for a given return on investment in their division.

The MIS activity is also organised as a division. Some 2,000 different applications are provided for all of the divisions over a range of computer-based facilities. Divisions are charged at standard rates for services provided, dependent on the volume and priority given, and are also charged on a time basis for systems development work. The MIS Division is not required to make a return on its investment but to cover its costs annually, subject to a budget allowances for innovative systems development work.

In the normal corporate planning process the company undertakes a strategic review every Spring in which each of the twenty business units submit their plans and make a detailed presentation to top management.

The time horizon is from 5–15 years depending on the nature of the business. Economic, market, technological and political factors of significance are described and the business plans for markets, products, finance, research, acquisition and capital investment are unfolded.

Members of top management question the executives during their presentations, at which the senior executives of the other divisions are present. Consequently there is an open forum about business expectations and the directions planned for the various businesses. The final allocation of resources by the top executive group follows the presentations.

The MIS Division is also required to participate in the strategic review process. Consequently each Spring the Head of MIS Division assesses the external environment, which in his case involves consideration of technological and economic trends and the possible pricing strategies of the computer industry over a 3/5 year time horizon. He considers the major projects in the systems field on which the division is currently engaged and updates the MIS mission statement in the light of known group plans. Like the other divisions he then develops and presents his plans for the services he expects to provide, the new systems to be made available, the technical facilities to be provided and the capital investment involved.

Thus the MIS review is linked into the overall business group strategies and Chief Executives from other divisions are able to question whether the systems and information capabilities will match up to their own plans.

In explaining the initiation of systems developments the MIS executive emphasised that plans for new systems are 'driven by the responsible line managers who set the priorities, not by the MIS staff'. 'In our business those who carry final financial responsibility also carry responsibility for the system. The MIS department does not dictate the systems that are to be used by the operating divisions. Our job is to co-ordinate their needs into an efficient and effective set of systems.'

This strategic review process also tends to spotlight the systems implications of any new developments that might arise in new products, new markets, new technologies or new acquisition in any of the divisions.

Following the annual strategic review there is an operational cycle which turns the long term plans into an annual budget for operating expenses and a project surveillance system for capital expenditure.

The Chief Executive of the Group claims that the integration of systems planning within corporate planning enables the divisional line managers to be responsible for their systems development efforts and the day to day computer based operations. 'It leads to less friction and more constructive discussion. It enables the strategic implications of systems development to become visible. It reduces the potential for political battles between the line operating divisions and the staff managers. Overall it means we are less vulnerable to expensive and time consuming breakdowns of systems and organisation.'

In this company the initiation of system applications is the clear responsibility of user management and they are charged both for development and operational costs. The MIS function provides a service, at cost, but is also responsible for developing and co-ordinating the information systems strategy which is reflected in the MIS mission statement and annual plans. In some other organisations the separate IS Division is required to make a return on their investment just like any other user of corporate resources.

2.   Systems Planning in a Centralised Service Company

A UK insurance company operates in Europe, North America and many other countries mainly through agents and principally in the life business. The company undertakes five-year business plans, which it rolls forward annually. This is the process which establishes the broad directions which the business shall take.

Strategically the Senior Executive has recognised 'fundamental opportunities for office automation, which in the industry will ultimately be the only route to survival and successful growth.'

MIS planning, under the direction of a board level Head of MIS, is integrated with business planning. Annually he reviews and publishes an outline of the philosophy behind the MIS plan, which is discussed with every executive involved with data processing right up to the main board level.

The operating plans of all the operating companies around the world come through the Head of MIS, who checks on the MIS contents and implications. A 'sign off' meeting with the President of the operating company and the Head of MIS is used to agree system developments.

The company also takes a very long term, ten years and more, view of developments, which is discussed at occasional review meetings lasting over two days. At such discussions, questions about the approach, for example, to data-base, the manufacturer's hardware, word and text processing, and office automation are explored.

User management, in the operating companies, is responsible for system initiatives, but the Head of MIS co-ordinates the corporate system developments. By having a board level executive responsible for MIS, the strategic implications and opportunities for systems developments can be recognised. The annually rolled forward five-year plan, and the occasional longer term review meetings provide a mechanism for integrating the corporate developments.

This company has recognised the strategic potential of information systems, not only for effective operations but also for the extension of financial and marketing strategies. Indeed, this is the company, briefly mentioned earlier, which linked its independent agents into a computer-based communications network, thus providing an important competitive advantage. The executives believe that further plans for office automation in their international offices will 'increase the competitive edge and improve our service to the insured.'

3.   *Systems Planning in the Operations of a Large Multinational Corporation*

The company in this case is in part of the automotive industry. The organisation operates with a series of geographically separate production facilities, which are co-ordinated centrally, and its products are marketed through a world-wide dealership network.

The annual budget for the central systems department is currently between $10 and $15 million. The top management recognise the importance of productivity in the systems department and the need for there to be a contribution towards group profitability.

The information systems strategy is developed through a long range information systems strategic plan which is updated annually. The policy of the company is that systems developments must be initiated by the line executive, who takes the lead and establishes priorities: it is not the prime responsibility of the MIS executive. Every significant new project must be sponsored by a line executive and the Corporate Vice-President who is also responsible for liaising with the top management team. In this way there is a sense of ownership of information system projects at the top level. Top management guidance is also obtained in establishing the direction of MIS efforts, consistent with the corporate strategy overall and management thinking on organisation structure.

Beneath the Corporate Vice-President level a user task force is typically created with the senior user management and MIS departmental management working together. The long range information system strategy plan is a written document which contains the overall plan and the specific projects in the systems area. It includes the following parts:-

1—The abstract

> A summary of the overall systems philosophy in the context of the organisation structure and management style of the business.

2—The introduction to the strategic plan

> A statement of the nature and purpose of the strategy and a guide to the report.

3—The current status

> This describes the present position of systems development ('where we are at present'). It gives an overview of each of the major systems that are operational,

from a user's perspective. It describes the applications with their related software and the organisation of the files.

It also includes a description of the technical, hardware base including telecommunication facilities and front-ending peripherals with a summary of the operational system software.

4—The projected requirements

A summary of the specific proposals from the user department executives ('where we want to go').

Each project is described in outline, from a user's perspective. It includes a reference to the organisational implications, such as any changes to the organisational structure or reporting procedures, effects on existing staff, needs for retraining, relocation etc.

Each project is set in the business environment and describes the purpose and objectives. In this way a post-implementation audit can be conducted against these objectives.

It also includes any relevant legal, security or privacy aspects.

5—The system concepts

In effect this is a description of the long term systems strategy ('how we get there'). The background to the underlying computer system is described and updated. The strategy for extending and changing the telecommunications and computer base is defined together with the financial implications. Technological trends are included where appropriate.

This section also covers the development of files and any longer term plans for centralising or devolving authority for the creation or holding of files.

6—Project steps and resources needed

This section identifies specific projects and allocates appropriate time horizons. The implications of manpower and finance are summarised in this section.

From this plan annual budgets are created together with the specific system development programmes.

4.   *Systems Planning in an Aircraft Manufacturer*

In the aircraft industry today the development of a new plane is often the result of collaborative ventures between countries and companies. Consequently transient associations and joint ventures are commonplace. Organisations tend to be task force, project orientated and change frequently. But, given the complexities of aircraft manufacture and the large sums of money involved, information is vital. Therefore information systems also have to be flexible.

As the Head of Information Systems in the company puts it: 'Our system plans are not blueprints. We cannot be rigid. Plans are made for changing.' He advocates a five stage approach.

1—Base the information systems plans on business reality, not on some grand design unrelated to the business situation.

> The plans must reflect the degree of instability in products and markets, finance, the labour force, technology and ownership (the aircraft industry in the UK is closely intertwined with government).

2—Establish the broad purpose for systems development— from the top management perspective.

> For example, to balance the aims of reducing costs, improving production or design team performance, increasing productivity or improving cash flow by reducing inventories or improving cash management.

3—Identify the core information areas in the business.

> These are the main sectors with information needs and the focus for system developments.

4—Keep referring back from information system plans to the business reality.

> If changes are occurring, for example, in legislation, labour attitudes, markets, technologies, products, what are the implications for systems developments?

5—Give system developments an orientation that is company wide.

> Recognise that the user departments and functions must see themselves as part of the corporate whole—an attitude which, he reports, many executives find difficult. There is a hostility to taking a corporate view when the orientation is toward specific projects and groups.

In developing information system strategies in this company the experienced and responsible managers take the lead, not the computer technologists.

The company also use external consultants to check on their plans, believing that an external review of their strategy formulation process provides a valuable contribution by being independent and also by being able to compare with developments in other companies.

5. *Systems Planning in the European Operations of a Large Multinational Corporation*

The overall management philosophy of this American corporation is to organise planning, product development, manufacturing and marketing on a Europe-wide basis. Eventually they foresee product development becoming global.

Whilst separate corporate entities are created for legal and tax reporting purposes, regional responsibilities are kept to a minimum. It is not thought necessary to have national staff groups. The emphasis is on a European entity under a European Vice-President, who reports to US Headquarters on the entire European operations.

The information system strategy must, obviously, reflect this corporate strategy and management style.

At the technical IS level there are five data centres, in Scandinavia, Germany, the UK, Holland and France. Two more are planned. The centres offer distributed processing throughout the company's European activities, and are themselves linked into a communication network. Management of the data centres report through the line management of the plant in which they are located, with a strong co-ordinating link to the central IS function. The annual MIS budget is $100 million annually and well over 1,000 people are employed.

At the data management level the MIS resource is organised Europe-wide and managed centrally by the IS function. Programming and systems maintenance is done in the data centres, which are encouraged to develop competences in specialist areas. For example, one centre develops the labour record systems that are used throughout Europe.

Given the complexities of organisational relationships in information system work, the IS function does not use organisation charts but relies on operating guidelines which describe the links, in detail, between the central activity and the local responsibilities. This framework of interactions is backed up by Europe-wide standards and procedures manuals.

The IS function is responsible for developing strategic plans for developments at the technical level and for co-ordinating requirements at the data management and organisational levels. The Head of the IS function links the information systems strategy for the European operations with the overall European strategic plans. He also liaises with his counterpart in the American operations on systems standards and philosophy.

Here is a company that is an advanced and experienced user of information systems, which recognises the strategic potential. They are now developing a system to hook all of their European dealers into an on-line communications network through which ordering, inventory enquiry, stock control and distribution can be run. They anticipate improved customer service, faster stock turn and better use of funds—although they do appreciate that it may be necessary to insist that dealers carry minimum, specified stocks, as the system could be used to reduce dealer inventory to the manufacturer's detriment.

6.   Systems Planning in a Global Corporation

'We are a global corporation in terms of our philosophy, our conduct in the world, and the management of our affairs as a company', explains the Vice-President (Information Systems) of this major Canadian corporation. He explained further how the information systems philosophy had developed:-

'There are a number of interacting processes which together represent a dynamic entity which we call the company. The planning, control, and administration of these processes constitutes the process of management of the company; for example

(a)   The market research—product definition—product introduction process.

(b)   The purchasing—provisioning—manufacturing—whole-goods distribution process.

(c)   The sales monitoring—sales forecasting—factory programming process.

(d)   The financial planning and control process.

Each of these processes has to be supported by an information system, or information flow which is the symbolic representation of the process itself. The information system in turn needs to provide the planning, control, and administrative data required by management to plan, control and administer the process.

In our company we are taking the view that:-

(a)   The company, overtime, consists of on-going processes which interact, each of which has to be planned, controlled and administered.

(b)   The processes are represented and supported by information needed to plan, control and administer the process.

(c)   The processes, the information flows, and the planning and administrative activities must be recognised to operate over different time spans and at different levels within the company.

(d)   It is useful to think in terms of strategic, tactical and operational aspects of the processes—and information flows—to represent both the varying time spans and the different levels of processes to be planned, controlled and administered.

Having taken this conceptual view of the company and its management, it became clear that a formal mechanism had to be established charged with:-

(a) Assisting management at all levels of the company with the formal definition of the process that a particular management is accountable for planning, controlling and administering.

(b) Assisting with the definition of the information necessary to support, or accomplish the on-going planning, control and administration of the process.

(c) Formalising the information into a disciplined data base and an organised information flow.

(d) Assisting in the definition of the management techniques and reports which, if used intelligently, will result in the effective planning, control and administration of the process concerned.

(e) Assisting with the formulation of a management structure (organisation) which will actively facilitate the organised flow of information, and the formally designed planning, control and administrative systems essential to effective on-going management.

In our company the Department or Division charged with most of these responsibilities is the Management Information Systems Division at Corporate Head Office, and Management Services Departments in our line operating companies. Frankly, I would prefer to use the term Management Systems both at Corporate and in our operating companies.

The Central Management Systems Department cannot discharge the responsibilities defined for it, unless it is:-

(a) Entirely service oriented. That is, its sole justification for existence is to serve the rest of the company by helping all other functions, via improved information systems, to plan, control, and administer the processes for which they are responsible more effectively on a continuous basis.

(b) Independent of any particular function or department within the company, so that it may serve impartially all, and allocate its resources to projects, over the company as a whole, in accordance with the priorities set by the Chief Executive and the board of directors.

(c) Able to identify and bring about interfunctional information flows, and means for their systematic establishment and control, to assure co-ordination among all the functional processes which interact in achieving the goals of the company.

(d) Placed at an appropriate organisational level within the company. Within our company at Corporate Head Office the management systems function reports to the President. Within our Operations Units (as we call our operating companies) it reports directly to the General Manager of each operating company with a few minor exceptions.

(e) Governed by goal setting and direction by top management. Without such goal setting and direction the probability that systems which are significant from the business and profit point of view is negligible, and the essential direct participation of senior user management in system definition and project management is unlikely.

(f) Finally, the management systems function must be accepted within the corporation as the vehicle for creating, defining, and implementing change. It has to be a catalyst for bringing about change, since, without change, there can be no improvement in either profitability or the manner and effectiveness with which a company is managed. By change I mean change in the patterns of information flow, changes in management structures, and changes in the method of management of the various functions and departments within a corporation.

Having defined the role and direction of the management systems function so that it can direct its resources to supporting continuous improvement of the profitability of the company, we had to ensure that the whole process and activities are defined by clearly stated cost-effectiveness criteria, so that investment decision on the development of new management systems (and computer facilities needed to support them) can be evaluated in a manner similar to any other capital investment in the company.

In this whole area, the key to successful and cost effective management systems contribution to the profitability of the company lies in the way we define the accountability for results of new and on-going management systems, in relation to the definition and control of management systems projects.

We have decided that:-

A   The user is accountable to top management for results.

B   The management systems function is accountable to *user* management for systems design and technical feasibility.

C   No systems work can be undertaken without an approved proposal; no proposal may be approved unless counter-signed by both the user and management systems management.

It is the role of the VP (Information Systems) to identify the strategic implications of the systems developments and to formulate the systems strategy, as part of top management.

7.   *Systems Planning in a UK Manufacturer with a Separate Systems Company*

In effect this major group of companies in the engineering industry has formed a separate, commercial entity to offer the technical level communication and computer technologies to the manufacturing and marketing companies. The systems company is self-funding, has return-on-investment criteria, and its corporate plans are built into the parent company's plans.

It is treated like any other supplier to the production companies. There is a separate salary structure and negotiations with staff unions are independent of the group negotiations.

The scope of the systems company's service includes:-

Computing services through their own data centre

Systems consultancy and development

on commercial applications

turn-key systems

stand-alone minis

word/text processing

micros

telecommunications

time sharing

Facility management of production company's data centres

They also offer access to a micro-wave communication network, electronic mail within the entire company, message switching between computers and a viewdata, information retrieval network.

The group of companies has a very formal, five year corporate plan which embraces the relevant strategies on disposals and closures of plant, new investments, product development, manning levels, joint ventures, financial changes etc. The systems company plans are part of the Group plans.

In addition the systems company must endeavour to co-ordinate the systems developed, at the technical and data management levels, in each company with an overall corporate view. This is achieved through the following process:-

The systems strategy panel	A steering committee of the Executive Vice-Chairman of the Group, various production company heads, and departmental heads and external advisors, which sets the strategic direction and meets five times each year

User working groups   Teams managing various projects-
                           user members with staff assist-
                           ance from the systems company

Company management   The executive teams of each com-
                          pany include an MIS plan in their
                          corporate plan.

Developing Systems Strategy—Conclusions

There is a need to think strategically about information systems; the implications are too widespread and significant to be treated as only an operational matter.

The real driving force in information systems, increasingly, is the needs of the business. Information systems supplement and change the way business is done. Consequently the way in which systems strategy is formulated must be dependent on the overall strategy, structure and style of the enterprise. There are no simple panaceas for strategy formulation.

In enterprises at earlier stages of systems development the responsibility for systems strategy tends to fall on an information systems function, which also takes the lead in initiating system developments. In organisations which are more highly developed, as we saw from many of the cases, a fundamental shift is occurring. It is the user managers who are taking the initiative and forcing system developments: after all, it is they who have the information needs. Data processing functions see themselves in the business of providing communication and computing facilities and staff support—not in the business of providing information. Consequently their function in the formulation of strategy is at the technical level as experts, and in data management and organisational levels as the co-ordinating activity.

The time horizon of information strategy is synonymous with that of the enterprise. For example, we have seen cases of up to ten years in outline, five years with more specific concern, three year roll forward plans in detail leading to specific projects in depth over three/eighteen months duration.

Organisationally the following levels may be involved in

the development of information systems strategy in a large, international corporation:-

Top management

> formulating corporate strategy, including a sector of information systems strategy which lays down over-all direction for the enterprise, with relevant policies and procedures.

Executive management—of user divisions, units and functions

> formulating their own sectors of strategy and involved in thinking strategically about their own information system needs.

Executive management—of the IS function

> co-ordinating the users system plans into an effective strategic presentation for top management. Establishing standards, budgets, programmes and project plans in line with corporate thinking.

> formulating strategy for the management of the corporate data resource.

> formulating the computer and telecommunication strategy at the technical level.

Fundamentally, however, systems strategy must grow out of a link with overall corporate strategy. If the long term strategic assessment in a business suggests that in ten years time there will be a place in the UK for only one manufacturer of that particular product, and that the industry will be responding to market needs by joint ventures and collaborative projects, then the IS strategy must follow that lead.

Reference

1. Tricker, R. I.: *Report of an independent inquiry into the Prescription Pricing Authority*: DHSS 1977.

8
Managing Information Systems
●some operational matters

"The aim is not to improve or optimise MIS costs; it is to improve the productivity and profitability of the business.'

DP Executive, USA

'Are we getting value for all the money we plough into computing? I tell you I don't know how to begin to judge these things.'

Chairman, UK Company

'They tell me computing costs keep coming down. But our DP budget doubles every year.'

MD, Canadian Company

The management of the information system function has become a highly developed and sophisticated process. In this chapter we cannot study the subject in depth. That would take another book—and many have been written.

Rather, the intention here is to give the non-expert senior executive an insight into the issues involved, so that he can ask intelligent questions about the use of computers and communications, and about the development of systems, with confidence.

Managing Information Systems

The economic imperative

For the past two decades DP budgets have been growing significantly in many organisations. An annual spend of 1% of gross sales in manufacturing businesses and 2, 3, 4 even 5% in the service sector is not unusual. Consequently the impact on the 'bottom line' in profit orientated companies and on cash budgets in the public sector is enormous.

Major costs are incurred on information systems at each level—technical, data management and organisational. Yet they are one of the most difficult areas to monitor, measure and control effectively. The cost curves in figure 8/1 are by no means atypical—whilst other costs have been brought into line to reflect adverse economic conditions and budgetary constraints, the information system costs have continued to climb.

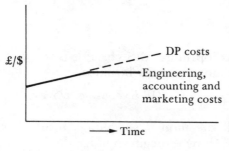

Figure 8/1

Moreover, the situation, far from becoming less severe in the future, seems set to accelerate. New opportunities in networks, data-bases, distributed systems and workstation automation in the office will continue to increase the information function's cost overall even though unit costs of data processed reduce. The growth rate could be massive.

New technologies in micro-electronics and telecommunications have been bringing down the unit cost of data-processing, data storage and data communication by orders of magnitude for some years. Indeed, whilst labour costs throughout the Western world have been rising by 10–20% per annum, unit communication costs have been reducing by 5–10% and DP costs by more (fig. 8/2). Such unit cost reductions will continue for some years to come.

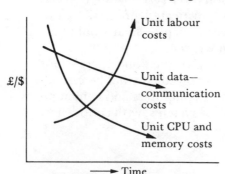

Figure 8/2

Whereas a few years ago there was a concern to use up any spare computer capacity, effectiveness now is not a function of utilisation. Costs are sufficiently low to allow spare capacity and idle time if that improves overall systems effectiveness.

With the substantial and increasing proportion of corporate

spending now on information system costs, there is an economic imperative to emphasise systems productivity, which will result in improved profitability in the profit sector and cost efficiency in the public sector.

Interestingly what is true at the level of the enterprise is equally true for the economic entity at the level of the State. With the acknowledged swing from manufacturing to the service and information orientated industries, wealth creation in future will become more dependent on information systems effectiveness; and increases in GNP come from improvements in information system productivity. This fact has been well recognised in planned economies, such as Japan and France, which have given the information sector special emphasis.

The managerial responsibility

Data-processing used to be carried out within the DP function. Consequently costs were incurred by the DP function and the responsibility for budgeting and control could rest with the DP function. (In organisations which are at the earlier stages of information systems development—chapter 3, stages 1–5—this is, indeed, still the case.)

But in those organisations in which the information systems have become significant, the information costs permeate the whole organisation. The managerial responsibility cannot be laid wholly on the DP or information function. Nevertheless, as we have just seen, the costs are significant and must be managed.

How is modern management to grapple with the allocation of managerial responsibility for information value and data costs? Whatever the detailed organisational structure and management philosophy, the relative relationships can be presented, conceptually, as in figure 8/3.

Between senior management users and system experts lies a coalition of interests. The challenge is to resolve potential territorial battles for the benefit of the entity. One of the important roles for an information systems strategy is to provide the basis for such a shared vision. Each sector must understand their responsibility and their place in the overall schema.

We shall find the three level view of information systems useful in differentiating the separate responsibilities (fig. 8/4).

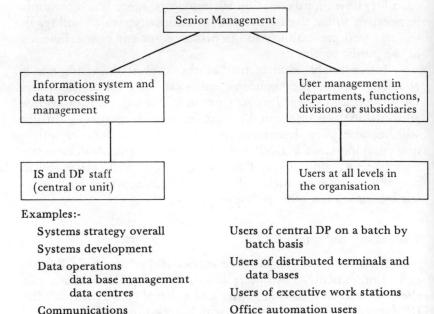

Examples:-

Systems strategy overall	Users of central DP on a batch by batch basis
Systems development	

Data operations
    data base management
    data centres
	Users of distributed terminals and data bases

	Users of executive work stations

Communications
    message switching
    micro-wave links
    facilities for distributed
      processing
	Office automation users

	Users of mini-computers
Office automation supplies	

Figure 8/3. What there is to manage in information systems

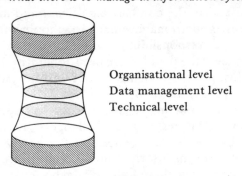

Organisational level
Data management level
Technical level

Figure 8/4

Management at the Organisational Level

Programme and project initiation, feasibility and approach

In the earlier stages of IS development, projects tend to be initiated and developed by the DP personnel for the benefit of the user, who must then be suitably involved and trained as part of the implementation process.

In more advanced, later stage, developments it is ultimately the user management which has to justify organisational initiatives and spending to his management. The basic responsibility for the initiation and justification of system programmes and projects lies with user management.

Yet the systems management has a vital role. There must be conformance to the corporate systems strategy in unit developments. Corporate criteria for evaluating system expenditure and the allocation of scarce resources must be ensured. There are corporate procedures, policies and standards to be maintained. Moreover the systems executive, either at the corporate centre or functioning in the field, may want to encourage certain system developments positively. He may provide systems leadership to the user line management from time to time.

The need is for positive initiatives to be taken, which are in harmony with corporate plans. How this is achieved in practice will, obviously, vary between companies, according to their own strategy, structure and style. A case example will illustrate.

The VP Information Systems, of an international (stage 7) company, describes the approach to project initiation and approval in his company:

'The need for a systems project can be identified within any part of the company, at any level, by the management of the organisation, or by the management information systems (MIS) staff serving that organisation. Authorisation to prepare a project proposal to meet the need must have the written concurrence of the management of the functional or operating organisation involved and of the management of the MIS department serving it. Thus no systems work should be carried out in the company other than under an approved systems project.

All proposals for systems projects must provide for full accountability of user management for the results of the proposed system within the user organisation. Each proposal will be prepared under the line authority of a proposal manager (who more often than not will also be the proposal writer). The proposal manager may be either on the staff of the user organisation, or on the staff of the MIS group serving it. The proposal prepared by him must be approved by the management of the user organisation and by the MIS management.

The approval by the MIS management also means that the proposed system fits into overall systems strategy of the company as a whole and is provided for within a list of priorities of all projects affecting all user organisations.

No systems proposal can be approved unless it contains as a minimum:-

(a) A clear step by step statement of operating or management problems the system is required to solve.

(b) Against each problem and statement an indication of how the problem will be solved by the system.

(c) A clear statement of what the solution of the problems stated is worth to the company, quantified where possible. Quantification in terms of management judgement is acceptable.

(d) A statement of costs
— to develop the system and install it
— to operate and maintain the system after installation

(e) Cost/benefit analysis using items (c) and (d).

(f) Statement of means which will be used to audit that the benefits claimed for the system are being realised.'

Practices vary on the justification of system projects. Straightforward, stand-alone, applications may still be quantifiable by equating costs against savings from reduced staffing. In other cases the cash flow benefits from reduced inventories, faster debtor collection, quicker service and so on may be identifiable. Increasingly, in complex, interrelated systems, ad hoc cost/benefit justification becomes a matter of managerial judgement. To use a metaphor—it is like asking the value derived from a telephone—and whether it justifies its cost: it is difficult to quantify but relatively easy to assess on a go/no go basis.

The processes involved cover:-

Analysis and definition—determining the requirements in detail

Design—specification of the system
—deciding the system structure and processes

Implementation—coding and programming
—training operators
—developing manuals
—conversion, cut-over, trial runs

Performance review—post implementation audit

Systems maintenance
and enhancement—repair and change

Systems development. One of the problems of advanced systems has been the growing time taken to get them on-line and effective. Facing increasing pressures themselves, user line management are less prepared to wait two or three years for a perfected system design. Various solutions have emerged.

On the one hand, off-the-shelf packages and design methods that are relatively easy to use ('user-friendly') have become more widely available.

On the other hand, so called 'prototyping' of systems is an approach which produces less than a 100% effective system quickly, but one which can be perfected and extended from experience. Users prefer to accept, say, 70% of the benefits in the short term and to learn and improve their system by operating it, than to wait for a 100% complete system in the long term, when their precise needs may have changed anyway.

Recognising that most system developments now have significant organisational impacts, and learning that people rather than technological problems now cause most of the development difficulties, there is a primary emphasis on user-participation in system developments.

A research study in West Germany discovered a whole range of complaints when questioning clerical users about office automation projects.

Employees felt that they now had far less opportunity to work with other people and were isolated in their jobs.

There were widespread complaints about the office climate, the noisy environment and lack of space.

Many employees also found that they were developing posture problems because they were not getting enough exercise and were confined by the new equipment to one cramped position all day.

Some of the new methods demanded more skill of the employees; others reduced the amount of skill needed. Well over half the respondents maintained they had not received additional pay for new skills they had learned. In addition, the great majority were convinced that their chances of promotion had declined in the new environment. Some 25% were even more pessimistic. They felt that continued automation would deprive them of their jobs entirely.

Participative design methods have been developed. The thrust is towards user responsibility with the systems experts providing consultancy and staff support. In some cases this shift of responsibility has resulted in adverse reactions from the systems analyst, who was once the prime developer and system expert, a principal agent of organisational change and privileged 'owner' of the corporate data, who now finds his power base eroded. Then the analysts themselves become resistant to change.

Occasionally user-designed systems are created with little or no staff support. However, care has to be given that systems policies, procedures and standards on such matters as codes, audit requirements, documentation, data-base methods etc. are not overlooked. In organisational terms, too, it is unlikely that systems designed by the immediate users would result in a reduction in the work force in that area: yet that may be an economic imperative for the enterprise as a whole.

In Europe, (Holland and Scandinavia are good examples) trade union involvement, in addition to user involvement, has become a necessity. Indeed in some Scandinavian countries trade union approval and support for system developments and changes is necessary right from the initiation of the development through to implementation.

Project management is an important part of successful systems development. Again there are many alternative approaches, from the very authoritarian to the most open-ended and participative.

The further comments of the VP Information Systems, mentioned earlier in the chapter, cast light on his company's attitudes:

'Each project which has been approved is assigned for execution to a Project Manager, who has complete line responsibility and authority to conduct the project in all its aspects. On major projects the Project Manager reports, in line, to user management.

The Project Manager is accountable to user management, and therefore user management has line responsibility and accountability for:-

(a) Ensuring the system meets the user's operational requirements agreed in the project proposal.

(b) User operating procedures and staff training.

(c) Installation of the system in the user organisation.

(d) Installation within schedule and budget.

(e) Successful operation of the system measured against goals set in the proposal.

The Project Manager is accountable to the MIS management, and therefore MIS management has line responsibility and is accountable to user management for:-

(a) Technical quality of systems design, and conformance to systems standards and policies. See Note (1).

(b) Development and implementation of a system which meets user requirements agreed in the proposal.

(c) Provision of computer and other technical level facilities (if any are necessary) for project development and for subsequent system operation.

(d) Completion of system design and development within budget and schedule.

Projects are staffed by personnel from the user organisation and MIS. All project personnel report in line to the Project Manager for the duration of the assignment or in respect of a specific task if assigned part time.

No project is complete unless both user and MIS management signed off for its completion.

With these policies and supporting procedures and management practices we are seeking, and in a large measure accomplishing, that only those management and information systems are undertaken and implemented which directly contribute to the on-going solution of operation and management problems as identified by corporate and operating senior management; which have full management direction and accountability for results; and which have an identifiable impact on the profitability of the company.'

Programming. The activity that turns the system, as designed by the analyst, into routines for the computer needs professional management.

Some managements fail to recognise the considerable investment they have in their portfolio of programmes. It is a hidden asset which could be worth many millions of dollars. The need for professional management is apparent.

In a typical DP budget 50 or 60% is likely to be spent at the technical level in providing DP and communication facilities; 10 or 20% on new developments, and the remaining 20 or 30% on the maintenance and enhancement of existing programmes. In one case reported by a contributor to our studies no less than 60% of a veritable army of programmers was involved in maintenance work. This later cost is often much higher, in long standing information systems areas, than management realises. Again there is need for tough minded management planning and control. Checks need to be built in after every 50/100 hours of programming and some companies give cash incentives for efficient programming completed ahead of budget time.

Another issue in programming is whether it shall be 'open or closed shop'—that is whether user departments or units should employ their own programmers or whether programmers should work, on contracts, from central DP services. There are arguments on both sides. Corporate structure and style will be the determining factor.

Post-implementation audit is another area in which the emphasis in the text book is obvious; but the rigorous operation by management in practice is often lacking.

Management at the Data-Management Level

As we saw earlier, data is a resource to be managed effectively; not a cost to be reduced. The increasing emphasis on user participation in systems and organisational development tends to give rise to a concept of 'ownership' of data. Users will refer to 'my information' and accept a responsibility for the adequacy and accuracy of input data when they perceive that it is the basis of 'their' information.

A data entry system on the production shop floor of a British factory was not used properly by the operatives, until they were provided with terminals from which they could obtain information of relevance to them. What was originally an entry to a system for 'them' to monitor my performance, became an input to 'my' information system.

However, there is a very important caveat to be made on the concept of the 'ownership' of information. Whilst it is valuable for users to associate their data inputs with their information, the property in much corporate data belongs to a much wider group. The ideal concept is like this:-

Organisational level
> the user identifies 'my' information,

Data-management level
> which is based on 'our' data—i.e. the company's,

Technical level
> which is provided by 'your' computers and communication systems.

In this way the important motivation of the user by association with 'his own' information is maintained, whilst the vital corporate, resource—the data—is protected and made available for all potential users and for audit and other purposes. The issues of data protection and security will be considered in the next chapter.

Data-base technology was oversold by some computer manufacturers in the 1970's and there has been an unhappy history, in some companies, of poor implementation, improper maintenance, inadequate use and bad management. But, given an appropriate information systems strategy, planning the data-base technology plays a vital part in modern information systems. These days the problems are seldom purely technical, almost always managerial.

We explored the nature of data-bases in chapter 4, on the potential at the operational level. Some of the managerial issues that do arise in practice are:-

- Lack of top management commitment and understanding. Often in organisations without an adequate information systems strategy. Policy changes are made which invalidate aspects of the data-base design, without management realising the value in the data resource.

- Lower levels of user management attempting to optimise the data-base for their own local needs, irrespective of the legitimate needs of other users elsewhere in the enterprise.

  In rare cases a data-base will serve a single organisational section. In which case organisational boundaries are not straddled, there is a shared language (and less need for a data-dictionary), no inter-departmental rivalry and common management. Usually the opposite is the case and political problems of structure and style, of ownership and responsibility have to be met.

  Evaluation in use is also difficult. The budget may be borne by one department, when the savings materialise in another.

- Poor data-base administration and management. There may be a failure to establish and enforce controls on data-entry, file updating and access to data. Very quickly parochial exceptions creep in.

  Data-base standards may be subvented, by users or programmers. The need to establish, maintain and police standards is vital; as is good communication between data-base management, programmers and users.

- Inadequate technical level support for the data-base: for example, poorly implemented distributed systems, capacity or design problems, inefficient interfacing with other systems—even instability of the entire technical operations when overloaded.

Data-base management functions include:-

- Liaison with top management and the development of a systems strategy.
- The establishment of maintenance of a data dictionary.
- User education, training and involvement.
- Development of user aids and support processes (e.g. the information centre).
- Establishment and maintenance of data standards.
- Privacy of data.
- Security of data.
- Audit requirements on the data-base.
- Quality control on inputs, storage and outputs.
- Liaison with technical level management.
- Cost effective and efficient administration of data-base operations.

Management at the Technical Level

The task at the technical level is to provide the communication and computer facilities necessary to meet the demands of operations at the data-management and organisational levels.

This means planning the computer systems strategy component of the overall information systems strategy, in the longer term, and, on a day to day basis, being responsible for operations at the technical level.

The computer (and communication) systems strategy focuses on the evolving needs for equipment and support software. It will be concerned, inter alia, with the philosophy of computing in the organisation—for example whether data is to be processed or made available on a real-time basis, overnight up-date, or batch processed, whether there is to be a central data centre, regional centres, distributed processing or application-orientated, stand-alone equipment; also with the configuration of architecture of the component computer systems; with the peripheral terminal equipment and, increasingly in stage 7 companies, with the whole technology of office automation.

Obviously there are many, highly technical issues involved at this level which cannot be pursued here. For example, in advanced applications, the manager responsible at this level will be grappling with:-

● Reliability   the flow capacity of the networks

● Upgrading capability   message switching packets

● Compatibility of   characteristics of data-storage media
    equipment   performance evaluation and
                                    bench-mark tests

● Vendor comparisons   physical facilities
                                    energy supplies
                                    controlled environment
                                    fire and damage prevention
                                    price
                                    compatability with other
                                        equipment
                                    support in maintenance and
                                        systems development
                                    spares
                                    reputation and financial
                                        stability
                                    training and updating

Given the widespread availability of a widening range of electronic apparatus, at a reducing unit cost, there is a danger of a proliferation of equipment as executives 'bootleg' equipment for their own needs, irrespective of corporate plans. The computer systems strategy, and the plans, policies and procedures that stem from it, give the responsible manager at the technical level the authority to exercise control when necessary.

Day to Day Operations Management at the technical level is, essentially, the management of production activities. Unlike the management of system analysts involved in creative open-ended design activities, the management of computer facilities and the data centre involves the administration of production work analogous to managing on the shop floor in a factory. Indeed, data-processing managers refer, in their jargon, to 'their shop'.

Measures of efficiency and productivity can be readily developed because input costs and resources and output performance are quantifiable. For example, computer system performance can be monitored on the various criteria; indeed many systems have in-built programmes to produce such data—

e.g.   down-time and malfunction
        connect-time on-line
        volumes of data processed
        file use
        central processor activity
        communications computer activity
        access time
        (in batch processing) the number of re-runs etc.

Other aspects such as auditability, quality of output, physical security and protection of data will be considered in the next chapter.

The ability to monitor efficiency at the technical level should not, of course, be confused with the measurement of effectiveness of the information system as a whole. Efficiency of the equipment does not, in itself, mean that it is being used to good purpose; any more than a well running motor vehicle implies a satisfactory journey. Effectiveness is a measure of user satisfaction.

Charge-back for computing services to the users is a matter of management style. In smaller, and earlier stage, installations it is usual to treat DP as a service to the company with no charge to user departments. Such an approach avoids the cost of accounting, is straightforward and can encourage use of computing and experimentation with new systems. On the other hand, DP then has to try to meet all demands placed on it: the only control mechanism is the DP budget and the user has no measure of cost to relate against his demands for service.

When the 'user becomes king' it is often felt that he should pay for the privilege. The use of charge-back systems can motivate users to make cost-effective demands on DP, and provides a means of assessing the performance of computing and allocating scarce computer resources.

In effect, by charging for the use made of computer services, a business-like link is created between user and supplier. Communication can be improved as a result.

There are some practical difficulties in developing a charge-back system. The pricing or cost-allocation mechanism is open to question—should the price be an arms-length, outside market price, treating computer services like an internal profit-orientated bureau? Should users be allowed to seek external, competitive services? Or should the intention be just to recover the annual cost of computer services in the price: in which case, what volume of utilisation would be assumed in budgeting and do marginal, new activities pay marginal prices? Should systems development be charged?

However, such detailed questions can be readily answered given a clear managerial direction on the style of control to be exercised. Essentially the use of a charge-back method provides a different managerial climate than the absence of one. Of course, a charge-back system does not, in itself, ensure effective use of data or efficient computer operations: that is a matter for managerial ability, but it can provide the mechanism for it.

The Organisation of Computing and Information Services

In enterprises where systems are in the earlier stages of development, it will be remembered, data processing is typically part of the accounting function or is a separate function with responsibility for processing data and providing information. As the user moves into the dominant position, the role of the computer and information systems function becomes service-orientated, providing facilities, and co-ordinating and consulting on user projects.

A senior executive, who has been involved in computing for many years, described the changes that had taken place during his own career--'I used to be the Czar of all data-processing: now I am Supremo of the systems. I have moved from line to staff'.

The interaction between the user departments and the information systems staff is clearly fundamental to effective information systems.

Steering committees are widely used to provide the co-ordinating mechanism. User and system management are brought together, with shared responsibilities, at different levels in the managerial hierarchy.

- In a medium sized Canadian company, in which DP reports to the Controller's function, there is a senior management steering committee.

  Its members include:-
  > VP Management Services
  > Corporate Controller
  > Manager Systems Development
  > Manager DP
  > General Manager of a major division
  > Controller of this division

  Meetings are held monthly and minutes widely distributed as a communication medium.

  The objectives of the steering committee are:
  1. To supervise the activities of the DP department and Systems Development.
  2. To recommend the approval of their budgets to top management.
  3. To approve and rank all new projects.

4.   To be a vehicle for sharing and disseminating systems information.

5.   To evaluate the level of service to users.

In companies which are further developed in their systems work (stage 6 and 7 organisations) there may be a hierarchy of steering committees.

● In a large British company systems work is co-ordinated by a three level activity:-

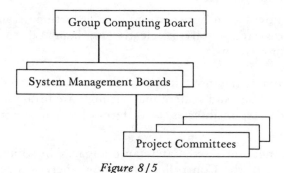

Figure 8/5

The Group Computing Board has group functional and divisional directors and senior executives from information system activities. They fix policy and steer overall systems strategy.

The Systems Management Boards each oversee a specific programme area: for example, production management systems. Membership involves the Director with function responsibility for the application area, Managing Directors of sites being developed and systems executives.

Project Boards undertake responsibility to supervise specific project tasks; for example, factory scheduling.

Computer Centres are run by operations management of the site involved; and Central Systems staff provide systems strategy, co-ordination and control and education and training.

Some companies appoint systems 'account executives' to act at the interface between users and computer services. Such people need to understand the information systems issues whilst being good at personal relations wiu. the users. They are involved with day to day operating problems, longer term plans and the development of strategy.

Each enterprise has to find its own solution to the question of how to organise the information system activities and to co-ordinate them with user needs, in the context of their particular corporate strategy, structure and style. In this chapter we have seen some aspects of the management in the information systems area.

NOTES

1. *Standards in Computing.*

Having read a draft of this work Mr. Ron Burton, of the Central Computing & Telecommunication Agency in the UK, commented on the need for further material on the importance of standards. He contributed the following notes.

1. Standards for the computing community and the people and organisations which it serves are becoming a matter of critical importance. This is particularly because of the increasing complexity of the whole field of information technology, the increasing interaction of systems, and the increasing general reliance on computerised systems.

2. The complexity extends to the subject of standards itself. In the field of information technology there are standards for hardware, for soft-ware, and for related processes and arrangements such as documentation of the development of programmes. The terminology is imprecise and not infrequently within organisations there are indistinct boundaries between standards, codes of practice, and general informal processes.

3. Something of a hierarchy of standards and standards-making bodies can be distinguished, i.e. international-standards promulgated by the International Organisation for Standardisation (ISO), national standards by, e.g. the British Standards Institution (BSI), and 'local' standards by, e.g. the UK Civil Service, which develops and promulgates standards for use within the Service. There are also separate standards or 'recommenda-tions' promulgated by the International Telegraph and Telephone Con-sultative Committee (CCITT) which relate to telecommunications and are therefore relevant to the expanding field of distributed computerisation and data transmission.

4. The present increasing importance of standards is also related to the history of computing. Until quite recently the computer world was dominated by a very few large suppliers (indeed some would say by one

supplier), who set the standards and the users then fell into line. That world is fast disappearing. The increasing number of users is being matched by increasing numbers of suppliers of an expanding range of different types of systems, and in this freer market there is a stronger movement towards user orientation. The user is more interested in interconnection, interchangeability, and quality assurance; to the earlier more monopolistic supplier these considerations may have been important, but his prime concern was to protect and extend his market position.

5. But although there is great interest in standards and users in particular think that standards are a good thing, there is also much lip-service paid to the subject. There is, for example, little in the way of concerted effort developed by users to promote standardisation. A main reason for this is that although all users recognise that increased standardisation must bring benefits for the computer community as a whole, these benefits will invariably come in the longer term in comparison with the shorter term effort and expenditure that is required. For example, even the DP manager most dedicated to standards will be tempted to take short cuts contrary to good standards practice in order to meet operating deadlines.

6. Because of this conflict between the 'general good' and the 'individual good', there have been efforts to give a stronger lead at national level to the promotion of standardisation. In the UK, for example, there has been established a group of committees with the aim of improving standardisation in information technology across the board. At the apex there is a FOCUS Committee under Ministerial chairmanship and based at the Department of Industry. Under this there are a Public Sector Users Committee, a Private Sector Users Committee, and a Suppliers Committee. Currently within this committee network there are moves to develop standards for Local Area Networks, to launch a national scheme for the testing of computer products against standards, to improve awareness of the importance of standards, and to introduce standards into public procurement processes.

7. In essence, therefore, although there is increasing recognition of the importance of standardisation in information technology, it is a complex subject which also involves a conflict of interests; and in order to overcome these constraints, a greater effort is being made by governments in the UK and elsewhere to develop more momentum on this front. Parallel with this the work of the more established bodies e.g. ISO, CCITT, BSI, etc., is also being developed more vigorously.

9
Avoiding Catastrophe
•the professional management of risk;
contingency planning

'My top management are most enthusiastic about computing but they really don't appreciate the strategic implications of what I'm doing.'

DP Executive, multinational corporation

'We suddenly realised—our whole business depended on that computer.'

CEO: US company

'I'm a graduate of the bloody-nose school.'

DP Executive: UK company

'If you don't think about the future, you won't have one.'

Forsyte Saga: Galsworthy

The strategic significance of information systems has been a central theme of this book. Failure in an information system can have a strategic impact on an enterprise.

In this chapter we look at crises that can occur at every level in information systems; and consider the challenge to management to plan for such contingencies.

Avoiding Catastrophe

Vulnerability in the modern world

In recent years, throughout the advanced world, managers have had to face growing vulnerability in their businesses: a greater exposure to uncertainty and risk. There have been many causes:-

- greater turbulence and more surprises in the international social, political and economic environment,

- the concentration of industries and markets—reliance on fewer suppliers, more market interdependencies and interactions between financial centres,

- dependence on fewer, highly skilled, often strongly unionised operations in one's own and other organisations,

- the interdependence of technologies, integration of systems and automation.

At the heart of many of these developments lies the modern communication, control and computer based system.

The dependence of the modern enterprise on its information system, and the strategic consequences of a systems crisis, are becoming more apparent. But few managements yet treat the matter with the concern they attach to vulnerability in other strategic areas—such as competition in markets.

It is catastrophies and crises that cause damage and disaster in information systems; and they can affect every level. Firstly we will consider some of the hazards that can arise and see their managerial implications. Then, secondly, we will study possible responses and management's responsibility to think strategically.

Hazards in Information Systems

There are four different types of hazard to be recognised:-

1. Physical catastrophies—fire, flood, explosion, theft, storm, earthquake etc.

2. Systems malfunctions—errors and malfunctioning of equipment and systems. Loss of supplies.

3. Unintentional human errors—mistakes and incapabilities both in systems development and programming and in data management and computer operations.

4. Intentional human action—fraud and misfeasance, wrongful use of equipment, sabotage and malicious damage, removal of labour, industrial espionage and wrongful access to data.

Physical catastrophies on the face of it, seem obvious.

- An American furniture company lost its computer
  and its customer records in a major fire. It was unable
  to recreate the records and advertised for help in
  collecting its debts. No-one replied. It collapsed.

But it must be remembered that physical hazards—fire,
subsidence, storm, explosion, earthquake and so on—affect not
only the home installation but remote locations, which may be
an integral part of the system. Moreover they may cut off
essential services such as electricity, telephone links, land lines
and micro-wave links, transport and postal services, computer
maintenance and supplies etc.

- A company housed its computer installation in a
  building shared with other tenants. A fire damaged
  the other occupants, but the company proudly showed
  how its fire prevention devices had protected their
  installation—until they discovered that the steam
  pressure, essential to the computer room atmospheric
  control, was provided by the tenant affected by the
  fire.

- A New York telephone exchange was destroyed in
  1975 cutting off all those telecommunication based
  systems routed through that node of the network.

- A South African company thought it had strong
  system security, until a catastrophe audit showed its
  dependence on computer links, over the public telephone network, between Pretoria/Johannesburg and
  Cape Town. This introduced a new factor into their
  thinking.

Now that computers and associated equipment have become small and portable, concern has also to be given to theft
of valuable equipment.

System errors resulting from the malfunctioning of equipment or its basic software provide few major strategic issues—but when they do, they can be significant.

- A US bank had to borrow $2 billion overnight, when a systems error resulted in a failure to balance its books. The fault was corrected in 24 hours, but at a cost of nearly half a million dollars in interest charges. Imagine the effect if the problem had lasted for a month.

As the Vice-President of another bank in the States has commented:-

'Investment in systems now totals hundreds of millions of dollars. A minor error in planning can cost millions: a major one could be catastrophic.'

In the past computer errors were the source of much amused comment—the payroll application that printed pay checks for millions of pounds, or the billing application that sent out nonsense invoices—but, by and large, such elementary programming errors can be avoided with modern systems design and programming procedures. Similarly modern equipment often has self-diagnostic circuitry which monitors its own performance and identifies malfunctions before they cause serious problems.

However, many of today's information systems are larger and more complex than the older, batch-orientated, single application systems. By their nature there is a need for a guarantee of continuous operation—for example, in an automated bank teller network, an airline or hotel reservation system or a hospital's patient information. Where there is a direct interaction with 'the public', down-time on the system is not just inconvenient; it can result in loss of business (e.g. airline ticket sales), an inability to operate (e.g. loading a wide-bodied aircraft), customer dissatisfaction (e.g. a bank teller network that is closed and will not dispense cash out of bank hours), or even loss of customer confidence in the business (e.g. where a major system error becomes public knowledge).

Nevertheless, in modern systems, it seems to be people who are more fallible than equipment and systems.

Unintentional human errors can occur through mistakes or in-compatibilities of computer and peripheral operators, systems designers and programmers, data management staff and middle management. Checks need to be built in to counteract such errors.

Intentional human action involve deliberate acts against the interests of the enterprise. They can come from within and from outside the organisation. They may take a number of forms. *Fraud and misfeasance* are, potentially, so significant that we will devote a subsequent section of this chapter to audit and anti-fraud conditions. A British study, based on the responses of companies, suggests that losses from information system fraud may not be as large as some people fear. But companies do not welcome disclosure of losses for fear of adversely affecting the customers' and the shareholders' confidence. They, also, cannot report those crimes they have not yet discovered. *Misuse of computers*, at the technical level can be internal or external.

- A British company reported that its operators had formed a private company to sell bio-rhythm forecasts, using the firms equipment out of hours. Most systems have some waste time with staff playing space invaders and printing computer portraits and slogans.

- A Canadian company found that a pirate terminal had gained access to its systems, using the public telephone network (through Bell Canada's Datapac and the GTE Telenet). The Canadian Mounties and the FBI traced the link back to a private school in the Upper East Side, New York, where students in a computer class were testing their skills. They succeeded in instructing the executive programme to give their terminal priority over the internal terminals and succeeded, effectively, in taking over the company's network. They also destroyed some of the data on the corporate files, which fortunately could be re-created.

Sabotage and malicious damage may not appear to be a matter of great concern. But companies in Italy, Holland and Northern Ireland have all been the subject of terrorist attacks. Dissatisfied employees have also used the information system—at the technical or the data operations levels—as a focus of their destructive retributions. *Removal of labour*, either unofficially or with trade union backing, has become a source of major worries, particularly in European organisations. Computer installations could also be subject to *sit-ins* by employees and others.

- The British Post Office was unable to collect any telephone accounts, anywhere in the country, for nearly six months, as a result of a strike by computer operators. The interest cost of the necessary alternative financing was substantial.

- An Italian university had its computer installation occupied by protesting students. The university was unable to function after a while.

The dependence on critical equipment and data files and relatively few staff makes information systems a particularly sensitive area for management and a pressure point for those wanting to exert power.

Unauthorised access to data or unauthorised modification or deduction of data is another area of major concern. We will review the privacy and security of data at the data management level later in this chapter.

Protection from the Hazards—Technical Level

At the *technical level* it is necessary to build the systems with sufficient robustness to provide a planned level of resistance to threat and also to be able to recreate data and restart after a problem. The threat of physical catastrophies is met by fire protection, security systems and tight procedures and controls on access and use. The check list that follows will give some guidance.

Stand-by facilities may be created internally—for generating electricity, duplicating communication networks, or providing additional computing capacity. Having compatible installations, however, does not guarantee longer term support if the overall capacity is not available. Such facilities are most useful in batch applications; they are not so tenable for large teleprocessing systems.

External back-up facilities may also be considered.

- AT & T has built a computer centre at White Plains New York, mainly to provide back-up to centres elsewhere.

Other companies, recognising that many businesses face the same problems, have co-operated to provide joint facilities, which vary from just a building with appropriate services into which equipment could be moved in an emergency, to fully operational computing and communication facilities. There are companies on both sides of the Atlantic which now offer computer disaster resources to major users.

- A number of British companies have pooled their computer stand-by resources and created an operational set-up for use if one or other business 'goes off the air'. They keep the location secret because it can also be used when labour troubles close down an installation in one of the member companies.

A crucial aspect of stand-by and back-up facilities is to test them, under realistic circumstances, regularly. When every minute may count, it can be disconcerting to discover that programmes will not run, that equipment is not exactly compatible or that some feature of the stand-by resource has been changed.

Technical Level Check List

Physical catastrophies

1. Fire, explosion etc.

1.1 Are buildings housing computer and communication equipment sufficiently safe?
Are there fire risks in adjacent premises?
Are computer rooms fire secure?

    consult experts
    rehouse
    install fire prevention systems

1.2 Are adequate fire precautions in place?

    develop procedures
    install alarms
    staff training
    regular testing
    simulate emergency

2. Flood, subsidence, storm, water damage etc.

2.1 Are premises sufficiently secure?

    consult experts
    building alterations

3. Theft of equipment

3.1 Are premises and equipment sufficiently secure?

    access controls
    physical storage of equipment

3.2 Are adequate controls exercised over smaller, attractive equipment?

    adequate procedures

4. *Recovery after disaster*

4.1 Are plans made?
    Is the stand-by equipment in the same rooms as the original?
    Does it have any spare capacity?
    Can back-up facilities be made available sufficiently fast?
    Do they have the necessary capacity?
    Are operators and support staff adequately trained?

    stand-by equipment
    back-up facilities
    manufacturer guarantees
    simulate emergency
    test plans and procedures

5. *Loss of essential supplies*

5.1 Are alternatives available for loss of:-

    electricity supply
    telephone supply
    land line links
    micro-wave links
    postal and transport services
    maintenance for computers
    communications
    terminals

    other essential services?

    technical study
    duplicate supplies
    stand-by equipment
    back-up facilities
    manufacturer/supplier guarantees
    simulate emergency test

Systems Malfunctions

6. Batch processes and stand-alone equipment

6.1 Do they have appropriate diagnostic and error checking capability? | test amend

7. Complex systems with multiple users

7.1 Do they provide an adequate guarantee of continuous operation? | test alter equipment

7.2 Are stand-by and back-up adequate? | seek guarantees

8. Application software

8.1 Do systems provide satisfactory error checking controls within programmes and in administrative procedures? | audit amend

Unintentional Human Errors

9. Are administrative procedures and controls in place to identify mistakes? — technical study amend

10. Are staff adequately managed? — management and staff development

   10.1 Selection and appointment

   10.2 Training and experience

   10.3 Supervision

   10.4 Motivation and leadership

Intentional Human Action

11. *Fraud and misfeasance*

11.1 Is responsibility for audit and other control procedures defined?	audit
11.2 Are operating staff positively vetted	hiring practices pass words entry codes
11.3 Are security systems adequate?	keys and controls on physical access staff identification consult experts in security
11.4 Are staff rotated periodically? Are holidays enforced? Is collusion essential in every case to perpetuate fraud?	audit

12. *Misuse of computer time*

Are controls adequate?

test
computer logs
controlled access
proper supervision
system entry controls

---

13. *Sabotage and malicious damage*

13.1 Have controls been developed to prevent unauthorised access to equipment by non-
information system personnel or outside
trouble makers?

test security

13.2 Are procedures in place to minimise damage by
internal staff members?

14. *Removal of labour*

14.1 Have plans been made for loss of operators or
other technical level staff?

14.2 Has consideration been given to possible effects
of strikes, picketing, occupations etc. by external people?

Protection from the Hazards—the Data Management Level

Data is a key resource, involving a major cost and representing a significant investment. Management of the data resource is crucial to modern business, as we have already emphasised. The loss of data can lead to the loss of the ability to manage. Wrongful access to data can lead to disaster.

Management needs to ensure the integrity, the availability and the confidentiality of their data. *Data integrity* concerns the 'wholeness' of the data—its accuracy, currency, completeness, unadulteration and reliability. *Data availability* is the ability to obtain access to required data, efficiently and effectively, when and where necessary, by legitimate users. Whereas *data confidentiality* ensures that only legitimate users have access to files; and that others are denied any opportunity to amend data or make reference to them.

Against physical catastrophies and system errors the means of ensuring data security, obviously, are similar to the ways of protecting equipment at the technical level. The check list that follows will provide an aide memoire. But, at the data management level, there is a special concern about security against human errors and malicious acts—fraud, theft, destruction of data.

There have been some spectacular examples of *fraud and misfeasance* perpetuated through computer and communication based systems.

- The Equity Funding Corporation of America was an entire company built up on fictitious insurance policies which were then reinsured. A data-base of bogus files was created, with a special programme to kill off a few periodically in line with actuarial expectations. Over \$2 billion worth of fictitious value was added to the company, which had to create more bogus policies to maintain their growth rate. When auditors checked a special programme—'routine 99' excluded all the fictitious records and produced legitimate ones. In the end a former employee reported to the New York State Insurance Department.

- A Union Dime Savings Bank employee embezzelled over $1 million by using an error-correcting routine, available by remote terminal, to move phantom balances between accounts. He was in a position to remove cash from the system.

- The Wells Fargo Bank in San Francisco lost over $20 million when a senior employee and a boxing promoter colluded to create elaborate money transfers between accounts, building up balances, until suddenly they withdrew a series of six figure sums—and disappeared. The employee was a trusted officer with access to a terminal and the possibility to transfer sums between accounts.

- An employee of the Los Angeles Telephone Company knew the codes that enabled orders to be placed by touch-tone telephone directly to approved suppliers' computer-based order entry systems. He ordered substantial equipment for delivery to himself which he then sold. When he came out of prison he set himself up as a security consultant!

There are other similar, often fascinating, tales of computer assisted frauds. Senior management should reflect on the thought that the most successful have not yet been discovered.

Theft of data is another important concern. This can involve the theft of programmes, which may represent millions of pounds of investment, as well as theft of data files. A particularly intriguing aspect of the theft of data is that, unlike most other property, a thief can steal it and still leave it behind—by merely duplicating a file. Moreover nobody may know it has been stolen.

- ICI in London had the only copy of some programme tapes stolen and an attempt was made to extort ransom money from the company. Fortunately the thief was a better computer programmer than he was an extortionist and he was caught running from a telephone box.

- It has been suggested that some airline reservation system programmes have been pirated. There is also evidence that the computerised customer list of a large mail order house has been copied, stolen and sold for a six figure sum.

- In another case a computer based information system was instructed to interrogate other systems, available on a shared network, to obtain details of competitors' engineering specifications and drawings.

Destruction of data—accidental or willful—is also a focus for management concern.

- The Hartford Insurance Company reputedly spent $10 million recreating data destroyed by an employee. Another employee in the Invoicing Trust Company attacked the tapes of GE dividend accounts.

- Militant students in Rome sabotaged the student record files, including their examination results!

- A subtle programmer, in a British company, prepared a fraudulent programme, then added a special routine— if his pay number was ever to disappear, when he was discovered and fired, the entire file was to be wiped clean, thus destroying the evidence.

In every example given of fraud, theft and destruction, proper audit procedures and managerial controls could have avoided the loss: but management of the data resource and their managers, need to recognise their responsibilities.

Audit is not a matter to be left to auditors. It should involve all levels of management and users in ensuring that appropriate controls are put in place at every level of the information system.

Organisational level	Systems and organisational controls
Data management level	Data-base management, input/ access controls
Technical level	Computer and communication equipment

Data Management Level Check List

Physical catastrophies

1. *Fire, explosion etc.*

    1.1 Are buildings that have data secure?

    Consider data in all locations:-
    primary data capture
    operational data held at technical level
    programme libraries
    tape and disc stores of data
    data in transit
    remote security data stores
    files held outside the information system

    1.2 Are procedures for downgrading and destroying data adequate and used effectively?

2. *Flood, subsidence, water damage etc.*

    2.1 Are premises and storage facilities sufficiently secure?

3. *Recovery after disaster*

    3.1 Is there a plan for recovery of programmes and operating data if lost, for whatever reason? — develop, test, simulate crisis

    3.2 Are back-up files and recovery procedures effective in practice.

System Malfunctions and Unintentional Human Errors

4. Have systems been designed to provide checks on data integrity? — check codes, control totals, administrative procedures

5. Are responsibilities for ensuring data integrity, availability and confidentiality clearly defined and are they carried out in practice?

6. Are procedures for ensuring data integrity, availability and confidentiality in force and functioning?

> e.g. acceptance of new programmes
> approval of programme amendments
> restricted access to files
> recorded access to files

7. Are documentation, data standards and procedures rigidly enforced?

8. Is the data-base professionally administered?

Intentional Human Action

9. *Fraud and misfeasance*

9.1 Is responsibility for audit and other control procedures defined?

9.2 Are programmes and analysts hired carefully?

9.3 Are employee relations proper?

9.4 Are jobs rotated and holidays enforced?

9.5 Are audit procedures enforced in every data area?
   input data
   operational data
   data storage
   data access

10. *Theft of data*

10.1 Are programmes really secure against tampering, unofficial use and copying?

10.2 Are data files inaccessible to other than the legitimate users?

10.3 Are responsibilities for data security clear and are procedures in place and working?

11. *Destruction of data*

11.1 Are programmes and data files secure against sabotage from outside the enterprise and from within?

11.2 Are procedures and organisational structures in place to reduce the risk of damage by legitimate users?

Some of the ways that management may enhance security include:-

- establish clear managerial responsibilities

  security levels

  division of duties to avoid collusion for fraud

  avoid any one person having absolute control over data files

- improve staff management—programmers and analysts

  employee selection and screening

  division of duties: limit know-how of the system

  independent programme testing

  procedures for training
  >   job rotation
  >   supervision

- develop standards, procedures and administrative controls

  documentation

  procedures for programme testing, acceptance, enhancement and maintenance

  codes of good practice

- consider security of installation, data-base and transmission

  log of computer use

  records of file use

  restricted access to equipment and files
  >   lock and key
  >   other security systems
  >   computer file access codes

  physical security—access, fire, damage, etc.

  try file penetration tests.

Protection from the Hazards—the Organisational Level

The more complex and concentrated an organisation becomes, the greater the interdependence of its parts, the greater the risk: as with any living organism. In earlier chapters we saw some of the strategic results of disasters in information systems— the adverse effects on marketing strategy as opportunities are missed, the effects on financial strategy as orders and customers are lost, the effect on production strategy as systems fail, even effects on acquisition strategy when systems are incompatible.

At the organisational level management need to plan for the contingent disasters in information systems. Has each eventuality been considered and the implications of a disaster on other parts of the business identified?

- The Personnel Director of a UK company reported: 'We centralised our personnel records to be able to make better use of our people throughout the divisions. Now the trade unions are demanding access to the file to compare labour rates between jobs and plants. It is affecting our whole labour relations policy'.

Modular, stand-alone systems have greater robustness than integrated, centralised systems. But, of course, they may not fulfil the necessary function. Redundant, additional capacity built into the system and back-up facilities can also enhance the robustness and reduce the strategic risk—at a price.

In addition to back-up equipment and facilities, management might consider the advisability of a back-up organisation— that is contingency plans with people trained to cover short or longer term problems brought about by a crisis in the information system.

Contingency planning is the process by which senior management cope with the uncertainties and risk in systems work. Essentially it involves:

- identification of the contingencies

    short term disturbances

    longer term continuing inconveniences or crises

    major hazards or catastrophe

- establishing the possible effects

  direct losses in the short and long terms

  restart costs

  additional effects on customers, personnel, suppliers etc.

  estimate the overall impact, on profitability or budgetary costs

- estimating risks—probabilities of the hazard occurring

  risk analysis

  managerial judgement

- decide what it is worth while spending to reduce the effect of the contingency.

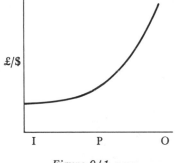

Figure 9/1

As more costs are incurred, the probability of loss can be reduced. See figure 9/1. But no amount of expenditure can totally eliminate risk. Therefore plan some funds for coping with a disaster if it strikes.

In identifying the possible hazards, management need to exercise some breadth of imagination. The check lists in this chapter give some indication. Professional experience can also be valuable, and some companies undertake a 'catastrophe audit' to underpin their contingency planning.

Establishing possible effects, particularly in financial terms, is difficult. But the calculation is, in effect, no different from the assessment of whether it is worth while to insure against a given risk. Instead insurance cover to offset possible losses is one way of coping with the contingency—for example, of loss of profits.

Estimating risks, is, theoretically, a matter of persuading decision-makers to state their expectations of an occurrence. In practice managers do not like committing themselves to quantitative probabilities, but tend to exercise managerial judgements in broad terms.

Strategic Level Check List

1. Does the organisation have a written contingency plan?

2. Is it the result of detailed consideration by top management.

3. Is it reviewed regularly in the light of changing circumstances?

4. Are staff trained in line with the contingency plan?

5. Have the industrial relations aspects of the information systems been thoroughly studied—including data clerks, operators, programmers, managers and external contractors and suppliers?

10
The Informed Organisation
•futures for information systems

'The confluence of data processing and communication may be such that it is no longer possible, from a regulatory point of view, to consider them separately.'

Federal Communications Commission, 1977

'In the affairs of men, there always appears to be a need for at least two things simultaneously, which, on the face of it, seem to be incompatible and to exclude one another. We always need both freedom and order. We need the freedom of lots and lots of small, autonomous units, and, at the same time, the orderliness of large-scale, possibly global, unity and co-ordination.

'... most people find it difficult to keep two seemingly opposite necessities of truth in their minds at the same time.'

E. F. Schumacher: Small is Beautiful, 1973

'Who is winning this battle?'
'We are.'
'Who are we?'
'Ask me tomorrow.'
Telerand

We have seen that more data, more readily and widely available, does not inevitably mean more information. We have emphasised that the aim of information system developments should be more informed executives, knowledgeable about the issues, threats and opportunities facing the enterprise; not merely the pursuit of technology.

But there are yet wider implications still to be considered. In this chapter, having reminded ourselves of the potential at

the technical level and the data management level, we review
some of the social and political implications that concern the
individual, the enterprise and the state. On the one hand there
is the importance of security, control and regulation; on the
other the opportunity as information systems promise more
informed individuals, more intelligent organisations, and a more
enlightened society.

THE WAY AHEAD

Only the future is really relevant to the executive: the past
and the present are but stepping stones to what is waiting to be
achieved.

At the technical and data management levels of information
systems it is not difficult to point the way ahead and to suggest
some of the uses to which the technology will be put. It is much
more difficult to understand the economic, social and political
implications and to predict possible futures.

Yet, ultimately, that is all that matters to people—not so
much what happens and why, but how it affects the quality of
their lives. That is why the management of information system
endeavours is so vital; and the development of information
systems strategy such a responsibility.

As the overall cost of the people resource continues to rise,
for enterprises in the Western world, and as the cost-effectiveness of data handling and communications continues to improve dramatically, there can only be further acceleration in
the development of information systems. The manufacturers
of equipment, the telecommunication companies—telephone,
broadcasting, satellite, cable—the system companies and the
suppliers of information have realised the potential and are
stamping on the accelerator. Companies on the frontiers of
information systems opportunities are set to surge ahead.

The Technical Level Potential

Over the next decade significant improvements in the
volume, speed and efficiency of data handling will be achieved
at lower hardware costs, although software support may well rise
in the aggregate. New peripheral devices and personal terminals

will come on the market, with their own intelligence and the ability to communicate with other, dissimilar devices. Interactive work stations will be widely used, as peripherals and communication media tend to converge, and become integrated and assimilated, as we saw in chapter 4.

Voice to data translators and voice synthesisers will be perfected. Telephone systems with their own limited intelligence, offering wider storage and search facilities, will improve effectiveness of operations.

Larger, cheaper chips will enable software to be built into equipment and readily updated. This will be useful for standard applications; although there are limits to the automation of the programming function. Programmer productivity is likely to remain a preoccupation of the '80s. Chips will also be a useful storage media for data, being thrown away when replaced. Various other storage devices, the video-disc for example, will provide new opportunities for storing voice, text and visual images in great volume.

In communications, complex networks will be created, both within organisations and open for public access internationally. Satellites will carry more traffic—TELSTAR had ten channels, INTELSTAT V has 12,000 and two TV channels—and will offer new facilities for international communication and, through stationary satellites, for local broadcasting. Only a receiving dish is necessary to tap into the ether. Ringmain telecommunication networks will proliferate within organisations, linking into external nets. Videotex nets will link millions of homes and offices with available data banks and, significantly, with each other, by the end of the decade.

It is interesting to note how quickly people accept new technology. The public has already been educated into using terminals, such as the bank cashpoint, and relying on electronically driven information displays, such as the airline flight indicator, without the expectation of personal service and confidence derived from direct human contact. This development is quite striking and sets the scene for further extensions in the next decade.

When data handling technology was primitive there was little choice. In the future managers will face a technological smörgåsbord, loaded with fascinating and attractive options.

There will be an abundance of choices. They will be able to do almost anything they want with the technology—if only they know what they, and their organisations, want to do.

The Potential at the Data Management Level

Once the office has become automated, the organisation ringmained with communication networks and the city wired, the potential will exist to store and transmit data in sound, text and picture between the component parts—within offices and enterprises, between organisations—including government departments, local administrations, professional bodies and academic institutions—with libraries, newspapers and publishers and sources of data; and into homes.

The amount of data already stored is prodigious. It is estimated that in the USA, the equivalent of two long novels of facts about every man, woman and child now exists on the soaring range of data-bases. The National Academy of Sciences, in the USA, estimates that there are 240 million records for people, living and dead, in the Social Security Administration alone. This amount of data is likely to increase geometrically.

Data-base management systems, now being perfected by manufacturers and introduced by user organisations, will enable widespread use to be made of this multiplicity of records. Structured query languages will make such systems 'user-friendly', enabling individuals with no programming knowledge and no detailed information of the codes and structures of the files to search them for their specific information needs. The computer-aided equivalent of browsing in a library will be feasible: so will the pursuit of 'what if?' questions.

The potential is even greater than appears to the initial glance. Communication of data between people and their workstations or terminal units can take four forms:-

One person/station	to	one person/station
One person/station	to	many people/stations
Many people/stations	to	one person/station
Many people/stations	to	many people/stations

'One to one' communication covers electronic mail services and conventional telephones—permitting the passing of specific

messages, in sound or vision, or lengthy text and pictures between people; perhaps providing a recipient with the right of
access to parts of the sender's files. Banking activities, such as
the movement of funds, enquiries and the payment of bills may
be transacted; goods and services may be ordered; insurance
arranged; and reservations made for theatre, travel or accom-
modation. Personal computing can be facilitated.

'One to many' communication embraces conventional
broadcasting and cable TV services; and existing viewdata and
teletext systems. These will undoubtedly be expanded by the
service promoters to include data on, for example, mail order
catalogue contents and buying guides world wide, reference
journals and abstracting services, the Yellow Pages locally and
internationally, information on geographical matters, weather,
news, facilities, entertainment, economics, industries, direc-
tories and so on.

'Many to one' communication, in one sense, is the reverse
of 'one to many'—the receiver's perspective of available information and broadcast services. In another sense it is more specific.
The information system could be asked to provide selected
data, gathered from a range of sources and locations on topics
of interest. The equivalent of the 'electronic newspaper'
would provide abstracts or the full text of material on
topics pre-selected or against a user's profile of information
interests held in the system. Access would be open to library,
reference, educational, medical, legal and other professional
services.

In another context, market research and polster services
could call for responses from a population of relevance to their
interests. Local and national governments, professional bodies,
organisations and clubs could call for *referenda* to elicit opinions
or call for votes on policy decisions.

'Many to many' communication opens the possibility of
network conferencing, bringing groups of people together over
the information system. Not only could this be done 'live', but
records could be stored and access made to files of previous
interactions. The minutes of meetings would become references
to file records or frames of visual records of the past.

Most executives will be familiar with the cliché about the
'information explosion': fewer will have thought about the

effects of fallout from that explosion. Yet that is what offers them the greatest threat and opportunity.

Thus we see a dramatic potential at both the technical and the data management levels. We should now consider some of the social, political and economic consequences that could affect the individual, the enterprise and the state.

Those involved in the development of information systems need to be sensitive to matters of systems security and integrity, data privacy and secrecy, the regulation of information systems and the need to balance freedoms of the individual with freedom of information.

Some Possible Consequences

Much work, in both theory and practice, is already being applied to such issues. Let us consider just a few aspects:-

In the wired city, the proverbial home of the Englishman may no longer be his castle. In the home, equipment would be linked into the network. Fire, burglar and emergency detectors would alert appropriate authorities directly. Temperature and climate could be controlled, equipment being adjusted to give energy conserving results. The security of people and property would be enhanced, as terminals would recognise authorised uses and react against illegitimate entry. Key, cash and tickets would not be needed.

But think of the need to protect against equipment malfunction. *Systems security* would be vital in such systems monitoring and controlling vital services. Accidental failure and intentional abuse must be prevented. Moreover, consider the knowledge about the home-owners' habits that would be available to the central control.

In the ringmained organisation, at the work-place, terminals would be linked into the information system that would recognise legitimate users, providing access to facilities, meetings and messages. Telephone calls, meals, transportation and so on can be monitored, and charged if necessary. Files may be accessed through the work station, books and records requested, messages sent, data retrieved from or accessed into data-banks around the world, action initiated, and so on.

What safeguards would be necessary? By monitoring such a system it would be possible to follow a person's movements, when and where he was, who he was with, books and files called for, telephone calls made, even his eating, and drinking habits. Clearly top management, users and developers of such systems must be concerned about *systems integrity*—ensuring that adequate controls exist to prevent manipulation and erosion of privacy, either by unauthorised persons or by malicious abuse of power by those in authority.

Similar issues can arise in the use of many data-bases, particularly those containing personal details.

> Customer records in a banking information system contain many details which, in the wrong hands, could provide valuable information—capital assets acquired, purchases and spending habits, payments to clubs, unions, and other organisations, subscription to magazines . . .

> Medical, legal, taxation, credit worthiness, job evaluation and police records also, obviously, can contain vital personal data that most people would want to keep confidential.

Personal data-bases are also proliferating within organisations. These will contain the obvious factual data such as name, age and address; but may also hold judgemental data on suitability for promotion and staff evaluations, and confidential data on sickness, attendance, education and training.

> One of the largest employers in the USA recently announced a centralised, corporate staffing inventory and personal profile system. It contained an inventory of work experiences, skills and education of all management personnel. Among other uses will be the automatic matching of moveable employees to management vacancies throughout the organisation.

Top management in organisations have considerable responsibility, and often potential liability, in the protection of data. It is as important to ensure that the data files are secure, as it is to ensure the safety of any other valuable assets.

Considerable interest has been shown in aspects of *data privacy*, throughout the advanced world. Norway has created a Data Inspectorate which issues licences before a file of personal data can be used. West Germany has set strict standards about protecting personal privacy; individuals may force disclosure of any data held about them and have it corrected if necessary. Such laws apply to data held outside Germany on people in Germany.

A number of European companies have adopted laws giving a right of access and correction to personal data. An issue of concern is that the legal definition of 'person' could include a company—thus giving competitors a right of access to files.

Britain prefers a system of compulsory registration of files, by their creators, to an independent protection agency. Legislation will provide for a public register of files, including their description and purpose, those receiving information, and security and maintenance of quality. People damaged by misuse of data would have a remedy through the courts.

In addition to ensuring that data held about individuals is accurate, it is also vital to prevent wrongful use. *Data secrecy*, ensuring that only approved users have access and use the data for approved purposes, is another aspect of data privacy that should concern senior executives. We saw in chapter 2 that information could be created for an interested person by combining two or more elements of data that, in isolation did not convey such information.

A data base of births contains records of all children born in a certain State.

Another file contains records of all marriages. Independently each file is innocuous. Access to both jointly would enable all illegitimate children to be identified.

It is vital to ensure that data, collected for one purpose, is not used for another if, in the process, individual rights to privacy are violated.

Credit records in a banking system, combined with bank balances could give tax authorities important information. Some governments might argue that the benefit to the State justified such exposure of the individual.

A survey conducted by *The Sunday Times* (2 July 1978) exposed the extent and the potential linkages of official files in Britain. Yet British law still allows the individual only minimal protection against the invasion of privacy and the wrongful use of personal information. The study showed:-

'... the interlocking maze of data-banks and computers which knows so many of our secrets. The Police National Computer is linked to 800 police stations which can pass data to radio units within 30 seconds. National Criminal Intelligence Centre, now being completed at a secret London site, may hold up to 1.5 million files on 'persons of interest'. Police forces may have Local Collators. Thames Valley computerise all incoming information. Home Office Data Banks record traffic tickets, prison and parole histories; new 'intelligence' systems are being developed. Recent surveys found disturbing 'leakage' from Local Authority social work and probation records. Parents have no right to see and check school records. National Health Service register is mainly manual; data on every child born after 1975 is computerised. So are hospital records of all patients since 1970. Doctors' and dentists' records are wanted by data-banks; the professions are resisting. The Department of Health and Social Security has 40 million national insurance files, computer linked to Department of Employment records, and Inland Revenue tax files. Customs and Excise have automatic links to police national computers and to banks and credit agencies. More than half the adult population has a computer identity code from the Driver and Vehicle Licensing Centre. Data from the last Population Census was leaked to Government departments. Post Office Postcode Index lists every house, flat and office.'

Each civilization, as Plato, Jefferson, Rousseau, Marx, and other philosophers have emphasised, has to find its own solution to the appropriate balance between the good of the State (the people as a whole) and the good of the individual. It is the classical dilemma between order and freedom, that we saw earlier in the problems of organisational design. In the late 20th century contemporary civilization has, again, to find an acceptable solution, in conditions of economic turbulence, changing social expectations and the potential of global and local information systems.

On the one hand there is a need to protect recognised *freedoms of the individual*: and not all states and cultures agree on the balance between individual, enterprise and state. On the other hand there is a legitimate case for *freedom of information* about some enterprise and state matters. The unanswered question is where to draw the line.

A British company centralised its personal files to facilitate manpower planning, job placement and payroll preparation. One of the trade unions demanded, under the UK legislation, to have access to the file to compare wage rates between plants. The company subsequently closed down the data base; reverting to manual records on a plant basis which retarded the provision of corporate wide information.

The rights of employees to information about corporate matters is of particular interest in Europe. In some European countries legislation exists to guarantee them rights of access to matters of corporate performance and plans that, in the United States for example, would be unacceptable to management. The 'Corporate Report', a discussion document produced by the Accounting Standards Committee in Britain suggested that every economic entity—company, charity, local authority, trade union and so on—which, by its activities affected the interests of other groups, had a duty to disclose information to those groups. The political reverberations of that proposal are still echoing around the hallowed halls of the Accountants' Institute.

The position of the EEC is clear. The Commission believes that throughout the democratic world there is a growing demand for greater public participation in decision-making, at all levels of government and at the place of work.

'Future Community legislation will require management to inform and consult with workers, and this will mean that greater prominence will be given to the workers' viewpoint. The final Community aim is that workers should be represented and have a consultative role in the supervisory boards of companies.'

Throughout Western Europe legislation and company practice has swung in the direction of greater disclosure, participation and, in some cases, co-determination.

The EEC Green Paper on employee participation recognises the developments:

> 'The current economic situation, with its reduced possibilities for growth, has emphasised the need for mechanisms that will ensure the pursuit of goals other than economic growth ... (which) can probably be secured only by the existence of decision-making processes in enterprises which have a broader, more democratic base than such processes often have at present.'

The right of access to corporate files by State agencies can also be a matter of concern. Should taxation or excise authorities be permitted access to corporate data, perhaps through their own terminals? The answer will depend on your view of the desirability of State or individual rights.

> The Occupational Safety and Health Administration in the United States has sought to require companies to release medical and radiation exposure records of their employees, thus providing the basis for investigations into breaches of safety standards. Such data could also be used by individual employees and their representatives to sue for compensation.

Whether such rights of access are desirable depends again, on one's view of the philosophical balance between the rights of the enterprise and the rights of the individual. The danger is that companies might not then keep the records themselves and, thus, eliminate any possibility of checking and tracing health hazards.

The right of access to State files by enterprises and individuals has also been a focus of concern. In the United States the freedom of Information Act grants such rights to call for data about actions of government and government agencies. Such rights do not yet exist in European countries, and there have been cases of European companies and journalists using the US law to call for information relevant to European company affairs.

The regulation of information systems is still in its infancy. Legislatures and opinion formers have still themselves to appreciate many of the issues of longer term developments at the technical and data management levels.

Control can be exercised at the level of access to specific data, as we have seen. It can be exercised over the creation of a system, as in Sweden where union approval is required before a system study can even begin. It can also be applied to the transmission of data.

Controls of *transborder data flows,* when information systems cross international borders, have become a matter of concern particularly to multinational corporations.

Canada, recognising that the cost to its national economy of having data transmitted to the United States for processing and storage in the central nodes of US information systems, has enacted legislation which effectively requires a duplicate system and set of records to be maintained in Canada.

As a protection to local employment and national companies, Brazil insists on government authorisation of every international data link.

Economic protectionist tendencies can be facilitated by information systems. Multinational companies are naturally concerned that legislation on data transfers across national borders may inhibit their ability to do business, and to control their corporations as they wish. The contrary argument, particularly from Third World 'host nations' is that they have legitimate rights as sovereign States to control the flow of people, goods, money and information over their borders. The interests of the people of that country are paramount and they should be able to prevent the 'exporting of jobs' and the loss of economic opportunities brought about by decisions taken outside their realm.

US based multinationals are concerned that some European nations are using legislation designed to protect personal privacy to inhibit the flow of data back to the US Headquarters of companies. National security, as well as national economic protection, may encourage nations to insist that data for running companies in their country is maintained in that country—and that they are not dependent on equipment and files in some foreign location outside their jurisdiction.

The Swedish Ministry of Defence put it this way:-

'The growing international data flow involves security and vulnerability problems ... in the event of an attack on our country a foreign power could benefit from computerised data on our geographical conditions, our production facilities, our power supplies ...'

They recognised the risk of accidental, or deliberate, interruption of data, particularly when it was transmitted via satellite.

Finally, in this brief sortie into some of the social, political and economic consequences of information system developments, consider the implications of a nationwide set of data networks.

The regulation and control of a wired world will clearly be necessary. Opportunities for censorship, for whatever reason, can more readily be accomplished through integrated electronic systems than with the independent, circulation of letters, newspapers and journals.

'Information is power' is an abused cliché. Strictly it is not true. Information itself is not power, but the exercise of power requires knowledge, which itself is dependent on information. The modern world has to rethink the balance between order and freedom in an information era.

Rethinking the post-industrial society

A number of scholars have been interested in these questions. Peter Drucker has suggested that knowledge, rather than capital, has become the central resource of modern production. Bell, from MIT, has described the new emphasis in the advancing world as the post-industrial society. But we have scarcely begun to think through what such a society might be like.

In the mid nineteenth century over half of the work-force was on the land. Today significantly more agricultural production is achieved with a minute proportion of that number.

The industrialisation and urbanisation of Western countries, which has occurred since the mid 1800s, now shows sign of changing again, as fewer people are involved in the manufacturing sector. The swing has been into the public sector and service industries; increasingly the move beyond industrialisation is into information related activities.

The relative prosperity of the Western world in the '50s and '60s raised people's living standards and changed their expectations. Better housing, wider choice of goods and services, and more opportunities to consume were demanded. In education a greater emphasis on initiative and inquiry, rather than on formal and authoritative teaching, may have led to a lowering of basic skills as some will argue; it has led to more questioning attitudes and a less deferential society.

The recurrent economic malaise since the mid '70s has not changed the acquisitive drive for material well-being for most people. High unemployment, particularly among the young, may have tempered expectations of conspicuous consumption; but may also have fuelled frustrations and led to alienation and a questioning of the legitimacy of conventional, contemporary power.

Professor Hirsch in a brilliant analysis of the social limits to economic growth argues that material affluence does not create an affluent society because the extra goods and facilities sought by the richer consumers cannot be acquired and used by all without spoiling them for each other. He suggests that alienation at work, deterioration in city living, the way relationships with friends and neighbours have become concerned with getting rather than giving, and the rat-race in education are all related to this underlying situation. The technocratic view is no longer sufficient, he argues, 'we may be near the limit of explicit social organisation without a supporting social morality'.

As expectations change in modern society, we face the need to rethink the relationships between the individual, the enterprise and the state. Old attitudes no longer fit the situation. Properly managed and adequately controlled, information system technology opens up new, attractive options.

The nature and locus of work can change.

On the adverse side there is no doubt that office automation and robotics in production process will cause massive re-training needs and the loss of jobs. In the United States studies have suggested that between 20 and 30 million white collar jobs will disappear or be fundamentally changed over the next decade. Some work could become more mundane and call for less initiative.

On the positive side, however, the advent of information system developments can create new job opportunities. Secretaries may be able to fulfil managerial tasks given access to executive work stations: certainly they can become an information resource. Managers may find less room for intuition: more need for knowledge.

Work may become more flexible, both in terms of the hours actually worked and the location of work. With information activities it may not be necessary to commute to a down-town location every day.

> An outside, independent director of a large corporation may be able to conduct much of his analysis of company and economic data from a distant terminal—in his home, another office or a communal work-centre perhaps. He could maintain access to changing circumstances in the firm as he travelled.

If people want, for example, to trade off monetary rewards for greater time in recreation or family experiences, or study and knowledge based activities, information systems can support them.

The exercise of control and the locus of power can change.

Appropriate information systems can facilitate the process of organisational devolution; or it can be a vehicle for centralising the decision processes—as we saw in chapter 6. Organisations can become more flexible, adaptive and transient.

Demands for a wider knowledge of activities and for greater involvement from employees, their unions, consumer groups, government agencies, stock exchanges and other 'stakeholder groups' could be met—once a need to respond to such calls for accountability were recognised by the existing holders of the information power.

At the local or national level, too, there is the potential to change the political focus of decisions by granting wider access to information and involving people more in decision-making, through referenda and polls. Such developments could respond to feelings of frustration, inadequacy and an inability to influence events that are heard in some sectors of society. Though often termed 'democractic' by their advocates, such initiatives would not necessarily improve the quality of decisions.

Although the development of complex technical level systems may seem to be a factor encouraging organisational inertia, slowing down change and making organisations more rigid; in the longer term information systems may prove to be a destabilising force in society.

Information technology can affect the way influence is exerted and power exercised. Traditional bases of authority could be eroded and replaced by multiple influences, which react too quickly, over-react or inter-act in unpredictable ways. Many of the conventional balances of power could be affected—for example:-

- With wider access to relevant data, citizens and similar 'grass roots' movements could be able to wield power against an elected local government. Similarly pressure groups and other lobbyists might be able to exert influence, through access to information, contrary to established opinion.

- The relationship between local government and national government could also be affected. On the one hand power could be drawn back towards the centre as information systems provide a force for centralisation: on the other hand information systems could be used as a vehicle for granting the local authority greater autonomy.

- Nationalised industries, public sector agencies and otheral federal organisations could find their relationship with the sponsoring organ of state significantly changed. Again the information system would be neutral as a force for centralising or devolving authority; but would provide opportunities for the executive prerogative to shift.

- The classical relationships between workers, and their representative unions, and management could also be rethought on the basis of a shared network of information systems. Collective bargaining would change its focus if both sides had access to identical data.

- Many of the negotiations which people have to make, from time to time, with bankers, tax authorities, planning departments, professional advisors and others have to be based on incomplete and sometimes inadequate information. How different such interactions would be if both sides to a negotiation had access to the same files.

Such issues get to the very heart of the relationships between individuals, enterprises and States. Much of the conventional wisdom is rooted in 19th century assumptions about the nature of the State, the nature of corporations, unions and other organisations, and the nature of man and the desirability of work. In a world which has become pluralistic such notions are open to question: and information can play a new and crucial role.

The Information Elite: New Responsibilities

If, as Norbert Weiner suggested, information is what changes us, those in command of the process have a major responsibility.

In Aztec society the priests controlled information. Only the Incas had access to the relevant signs; only they could interpret the portends. The information elite controlled the law and the people.

In 18th century London business information passed from person to person in the coffee houses, with carefully penned letters and printed pamphlets. But access to the coffee house conversation depended on being a member of the information elite; and value from the printed word needed the ability to read.

Now in the late 20th century world, who forms the information elite? What are the qualifications for membership? What qualities, what knowledge, what position determines the power of those who control information? Indeed, with the plethora of modern information and communication technology, do we know who can decide?

There are no panaceas or 'golden rules' for successful system developments. In earlier chapters we suggested that organisations went through stages in developing information systems and their organisation. But such a 'stages theory' is a device for focusing the attention, not a set of inevitable rules. Rather we have to recognise that information system developments are contingent on the organisational circumstances. Organisations are dynamic. Change must be planned. Consequently systems development, organisational development and management development must move hand in hand. The implications, for most enterprises, have yet to be recognised.

In this book we have emphasised the responsibility of those leading the modern enterprise and the modern state. Technology is not the issue: it is already well ahead of management's ability to understand the implications and imagine the alternatives, and the gap is widening fast. The challenge to management is to appreciate the issues and the opportunities: recognise the new competences they must acquire. Nor is it a matter of professional management of a computer support function. The issues are at top management level. Every enterprise should have its information systems strategy.

Some organisations have taken this perspective. They recognise that changes in strategy, organisation structure and management style must be planned: and planned as part of a longer term information system strategy. But the number of such successful enterprises is woefully small.

A leading consultant in the United States said recently to the author:

'I am amazed at how little systems strategy exists in the US. In London the view is that America is years ahead: but I am unable to find it. There *are* visionaries, it is true, but there is a significant absence of real strategic thinking about information systems.'

Technology can offer the potential; but only top management can provide the leadership. Efficient computer operations and a functioning computer steering committee are not enough. Strategy formulation calls for men and women of vision—able to imagine possible futures for their enterprise. This applies as much in information systems strategy as in marketing, acquisition and financial strategies. The need is for innovation, creativity and a shared vision at the top.

Communication and computer equipment at the technical level and the resources of data at the data management level promise great opportunities. But in that promise they are neutral. They may be forces for success or failure, for good or bad, in an organisation and in a society.

We are witnessing, indeed we are part of, a social metamorphosis. We might fail to respond to new social expectations, realistic new economic opportunities, and possible political initiatives; we might contribute to an excessively specialised society with little place for the generalist; we could encourage a non-verbal society, stunned into insensitivity by a bombardment of data. We could slip towards a domination by central authority. Essential freedoms could be eroded and ultimately lost.

But we could have more genuinely informed individuals, more intelligent organisations and a more enlighted society. It should not be left to chance.

Index